How Can I Stop?

Breaking my deviant cycle

a guided workbook for clients in treatment

by Laren Bays, Robert Freeman-Longo

& Diane Montgomery-Logan

SaferSocietyPress

PO BOX 340 • BRANDON, VT 05733-0340
PHONE: (802) 247-3132

Design: Whitman Communications, Inc.

Editors: Euan Bear & Fay Honey Knopp

ISBN: 1-884444-26-1

Order from:

The Safer Society Press
PO Box 340
Brandon, VT 05733-0340
(802) 247-3132

$12.00
U.S. Funds only
Vermont residents, please add sales tax

Acknowledgments

The ideas found in the journal section of this workbook are adaptations of those of Rita K. MacDonald, former director of the Vermont Treatment Program for Sexual Aggressors, and William D. Pithers, PhD, Director of the Vermont Center for the Prevention and Treatment of Sexual Abuse, from "Self-monitoring to Identify High-risk Situations," in *Relapse Prevention with Sex Offenders*, edited by Richard Laws, PhD (Guilford Press, 1989). Thanks to William Pithers for his careful reading and insightful comments on the workbook manuscript.

Contents

Introduction

CONGRATULATIONS AND THANK YOU for acquiring *How Can I Stop? Breaking My Deviant Cycle*. This guided self-help workbook is Number Three in the Sex Offenders' Studies (SOS) Series that has been developed to help people who have problems with sexuality and aggression. We strongly recommend that before beginning this workbook you read and complete the first two workbooks in the series: *Who Am I and Why Am I in Treatment?* (Number One) and *Why Did I Do It Again?* (Number Two). If you don't read the workbooks or chapters in order, you may feel confused, lost in the material, or discouraged.

In *Who Am I?* you read a brief overview about behavioral cycles and completed assignments that helped you identify some of your own cycles. *Why Did I Do It Again?* guided you step-by-step through the links and chains of your own deviant cycle, pointing out where each behavior pattern begins, where it leads, and how it is linked to other behavior patterns that end in abusive sexual acts. *Why Did I?* also introduced the concepts and timing of effective interventions to stop your aggressive behavior. *How Can I Stop?* teaches you some of the techniques mentioned in *Why Did I?*; with these techniques, you can stop problem behaviors and start healthy ones.

Each chapter in this workbook contains homework assignments to help you better understand the material and practice what you have learned. If you do not understand any assignment, ask your therapist, group, or a close friend. We recommend that you not write in this workbook; keep a separate notebook for writing each of your assignments. Review your homework assignments with your therapist, group, or friend.

We strongly recommend that you join a treatment program for sex offenders. However, in many places specialized treatment is not available. If you must work on your own, share your assignments with a friend or someone else you can trust to give you accurate, honest feedback.

Again, we congratulate you on your efforts to help yourself through treatment. We wish you courage and determination in your treatment program and in completing this workbook. If you are working on your own, we hope these workbooks will be a useful tool for you and that you will continue to work at making changes in your life. GOOD LUCK!

Laren Bays
Portland, Oregon

Rob Freeman-Longo
Brandon, Vermont

Diane Montgomery-Logan
Burlington, Vermont

1.
Building My New Foundations for Change

ULTIMATELY THERE IS ONE VITAL REASON for you to be in treatment: you have harmed people by making them victims of your deviant sexual behavior. The effects of abusive sexuality on victims go deep and last long. In a good treatment program you learn in detail about the effects of your crimes. You *must* understand what your victims have experienced and are experiencing because of your crimes. Progress in therapy is *not* based on your level of satisfaction with yourself and your life. It is *not* based on how well you communicate. It is *not* based on your understanding. **Progress is based on your not having one more victim.** Having no more victims is the only measure of whether you are being successful. Having one more victim means you have failed.

The goal of this workbook is to help you build new foundations for changing your behavior so you will not victimize anyone else. Foundations of understanding support your use of new techniques to keep you from reoffending.

Relapse Prevention

The formal system of preventing a reoffense is called *Relapse Prevention* (RP). It is a self-control and maintenance program based on the idea that *you* are responsible for creating your deviant behaviors—and that *you* are also capable of stopping them. The RP model teaches you how to figure out when you are starting your deviant cycle or are at risk to reoffend. It shows you how to use the information you've learned about yourself and your deviant cycle to plan for and cope with situations that can lead to relapse. As you practice RP you will gain new healthy behaviors to substitute for old destructive ones. Your goal is to end your deviant, criminal, and abusive behaviors.

Risk Factors

A *risk factor* is any place, thought, behavior, feeling, or memory that could make you more likely to reoffend. When considering if something is a risk factor, ask yourself, "If the worst happened right now, would I be more likely to reoffend?" If the answer is yes, it is a risk factor, and you need to intervene to stop yourself from going further. Encountering a risk factor does not mean that you *will* reoffend again; it is only a warning sign that you could start sliding into deviant behavior. If you know that you're getting a little off your healthy path, you can use an intervention, correct yourself, and prevent your relapse.

Risk factors can be internal or external. Internal risk factors include emotions, thoughts, beliefs, or behaviors that signal that you are heading for trouble. Some common risk factors include: greed, anger, self-pity, deviant fantasies, masturbation as an outlet for loneliness or anger, loneliness, tiredness, over-eating, over-spending, or over-working. External risk factors are usually certain places or other stimuli. An X-rated movie theater, a job with children, a job that requires lots of unsupervised driving, or friends who use drugs or alcohol all may be risk factors.

Links

A series of *links* join to form a chain. Your deviant cycle is held together by small links of feelings, thoughts, behaviors, and events or environments (some of which may be risk factors). One link leads to the next, letting you choose to put yourself into less and less healthy states. If you are a rapist, aimless driving may link your feeling of boredom with looking for a victim. If you are a child molester, seeing an ad on television may be linked by your deviant fantasies to acting out sexually with children.

Because links are different for each person, it is important that you learn what your links are. Links can be very hard to see since they can be common emotions or activities connecting the parts of your deviant cycle. Everyday activities or feelings may be signs that you have progressed further into your deviant cycle. What is a problem for you may not be a problem for someone else. Being aware of your links will help you break them before you are so deeply into your cycle that you are in danger of lapsing or even reoffending.

Seemingly Unimportant Decisions

Seemingly Unimportant Decisions (SUDs) are links you use to progress from one risk factor to another. A Seemingly Unimportant Decision is a small decision which *at first* seems unimportant. For example, when you go out for a walk, you may make a Seemingly Unimportant Decision in deciding which way to turn. On the surface it does not matter in which direction you go, so you choose the right hand street. However, if you had thought about the adult bookstores you would pass two blocks down the right hand street, you would have seen that it would have made a big difference. In this example, turning right was a SUD. At the moment you turned, it did not seem to make a difference. Yet it is a decision that could easily lead you toward an external risk factor (the bookstores) and into your deviant cycle (using pornography). When you know the pattern of your deviant behavior, the links and chains in your cycle, and your risk factors, you are less likely to make a SUD that brings you closer to reoffending.

Lapse Versus Relapse

No matter how strong your desire to maintain an offense-free life, you will have periods when you don't do as well as you would like to. There will be times when you don't perform perfectly and engage in a risky behavior—when it seems like you've taken three steps forward and one back. A *lapse* is when you slide back into the beginnings of your deviant cycle *without reoffending*. A lapse happens when you're not

paying close attention and you begin to creep back into deviant behavior. For example, when you know pornography is part of your deviant pattern, picking up a *Playboy* magazine lying around at work is a *lapse*. You have not *reoffended* (relapsed) but you are on the way. Another example of a lapse: you know it is wrong for you to be around children, but you open the door and talk to the two girls selling Girl Scout cookies. You are closer to a relapse (reoffense) talking to the children than if you were not talking to them. A *lapse* is most likely to occur in a *high-risk situation*. The interventions you learn in this workbook are for every type of risk situation.

A *relapse* is a reoffense, committing another sexual act with a victim. Anyone who relapses (reoffends) has already *lapsed* several times on his way toward reoffending.

Abstinence Violation Effect

Abstinence means not using or doing something. You may decide to abstain from drugs, pornography, sex, meat, alcohol, or anything you desire. *Violation* means breaking a rule. *The Abstinence Violation Effect* (AVE) describes how you feel when you've broken your promise to give something up (lapsed). When you're experiencing AVE, you feel like a failure and want to give up completely ("I blew it, it's no use, I'll never change"). You may think you might as well go all the way into your offending behavior. For example, men who stop drinking often backslide, have one more drink, then give up and go on a binge.

AVE makes it easier for you to relapse by encouraging you to give yourself permission to reoffend. You are most likely to notice this effect when you are deep in your cycle, when high-risk factors are all around you. By knowing in advance that you will make mistakes, lapse, and feel like giving up, you can save yourself and your potential victim by using an emergency escape (see Chapter Two). Knowing that you never have to give up controlling your deviant behavior will help you if you come close to reoffending. Not giving up always helps your potential victims and helps you feel better about yourself.

The diagram below puts all these elements together to show how RP works.[1]

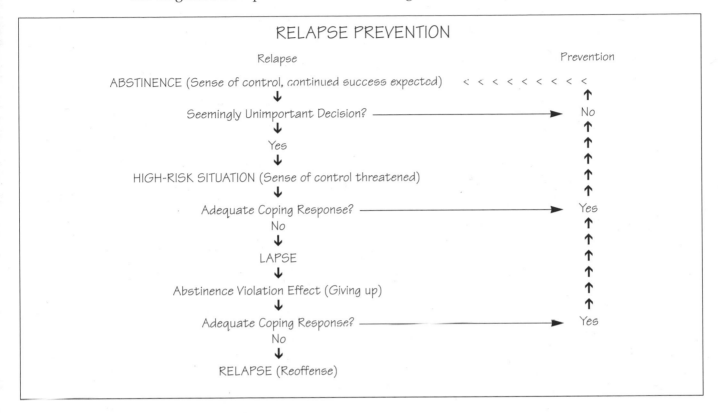

RELAPSE PREVENTION

Relapse   Prevention

ABSTINENCE (Sense of control, continued success expected) < < < < < < < < <
        ↓   ↑
Seemingly Unimportant Decision? ————————————————————————→   No
        ↓   ↑
       Yes   ↑
        ↓   ↑
HIGH-RISK SITUATION (Sense of control threatened)   ↑
        ↓   ↑
Adequate Coping Response? ——————————————————————————————→   Yes
       No   ↑
        ↓   ↑
      LAPSE   ↑
        ↓   ↑
Abstinence Violation Effect (Giving up)   ↑
        ↓   ↑
Adequate Coping Response? ——————————————————————————————→   Yes
       No
        ↓
RELAPSE (Reoffense)

You want *never* to reach the bottom on this diagram. Using the interventions you learn in this workbook will take you over to the right hand path leading back up to abstinence and continued success.

Interventions

Interventions are techniques you use to stop your bad habits, thoughts, feelings, or behaviors before you act out deviant sexual behavior. Interventions break the links in your deviant cycle and get you out of high-risk situations by substituting healthy thoughts, feelings, and behaviors for your deviant ones. They help you *prevent relapse*. On the RP diagram, *interventions* are the "adequate coping responses" that help you stay confident, in control, and offense-free.

You must make the intervention, no one else can do it for you. Remember, an intervention is not just stopping deviancy, it is also starting a healthy behavior.

Taking part in positive activities is one part of breaking a deviant cycle. As you read and apply the information in this workbook, focus on the question, "What can I DO that is healthy?" When you learn new, healthy (and sometimes pleasurable) behaviors while breaking your deviant cycle, your work will be easier and you will make more progress.

Foundations for Good Interventions

A few conditions lay a solid foundation for good interventions:

Honesty. Honesty is essential for a healthy life and good interventions. Without a basic commitment to honesty you end up lying. Small lies lead to large lies and set you on the road to deviancy. A sex offender who says that he is going to change without first making a basic commitment to be honest has already

---

[1]Adapted from Pithers, W.D., Kashima, K.M., Cumming, G.F., Beal, L.S., & Buell, M.M. (1988). Relapse prevention of sexual aggression. In R. A. Prentky & V.R. Quinsey (Eds.). *Human sexual aggression: Current perspectives* (p. 248). Annals of the New York Academy of Sciences Vol. 528. New York: The New York Academy of Sciences.

failed. Being honest means that you can tell the truth about what you have done in the past and what you are doing now, even when the truth is painful to you. It means being honest with yourself and everyone else with whom you come into contact. If you think that you can be honest with yourself and lie to others, you are mistaken. Lying slowly rots your good intentions and destroys the good person you have the power to be. When you lie, it gradually becomes a way of life.

Honesty is the most important quality you need to change your deviant behavior. Being a liar readies you to reoffend. Trying to develop interventions while you are still lying to yourself is setting yourself up for failure. "Compartmentalizing" (review Chapter Eight of SOS Two to remind yourself how this dynamic operates) is another form of lying to yourself by focusing only on the good parts of yourself and pretending that they make up for your offenses.

Total honesty is a sledgehammer you can use to break the links of your deviant cycle. Your deviant links and chains cannot stand up under the impact of totally honest thinking.

A willingness to change. You must be willing to look *honestly* at your problems, ways of thinking, old habits, weaknesses, and imperfections. Then you must be willing to work to give them up. Without your willingness to change, all techniques and insight are useless. If you feel anger, jealousy, greed, envy, or deviant sexual desire, being honest about what you feel is important. But you also must be willing to *change* the way you feel. For example, if you like to manipulate others, being honest about this feeling is important. If you deny you have those feelings, how could you change them? Once you admit your experience, you must do something about it. Unfortunately, Ivan the Intimidator was not willing to make changes:

My name is Ivan, and I've been in a maximum security prison for torturing and raping a woman. In my therapy group I learned that I could speak openly about my crimes, my feelings, and my thoughts. I really had that therapist going: I'd speak up in group and look right at a guy I wanted to scare while I told all the gory details of how I tortured that woman and raped her. My therapist thought I was doing really well with my "disclosure." But the other guys in group knew I was threatening them and they were scared. Man, it made me feel powerful, at least for awhile. But, you know, I never really got anywhere in that group. There wasn't anything I wanted to change.

Many men who first hear about being honest (and expressing their feelings) think that it simply means they should tell everyone when they are angry or irritated with them and that others should automatically comply and change their behavior. Talking honestly about your feelings *is* better than letting them build up inside, explode, and hurt others. But talking honestly about how you feel is not enough, *you must want to change your problem feelings*. Consider Grouchy Greg's case:

My name is Greg. You SOBs are a bunch of slimeballs. And it's okay for me to say so because my sex-offender group said I should be honest about my feelings. First I thought it was great! But you toilet heads got me in a lot of trouble! I went to my shop trying to be honest, and I told every guy there just what I thought of him. They're all a bunch of dickheads. I got fired for trying to be honest!

Expressing negative feelings over and over just makes you an honest grouch whom no one wants to be around. No one likes a chronic complainer. Talking honestly is important but you must also be willing to change. You must learn to turn your negative feelings into positive ones, your anger into humor, your irritation into patience, your greed into generosity.

Skill. If you are honest with yourself and others and are willing to change but do not know how to make the right changes, you are stuck. It is like trying to sit on a stool that has only two legs. No matter how hard you try, you keep falling over. Problem-solving skills are the tools you can use to keep yourself in balance by stopping your deviant behavior. To build a house, it is not enough to have plans and the desire; you also must have the tools. In this volume you will learn about several tools, specific techniques that can help you stop acting out.

Timing. Having the right tools is still not enough. You must learn when to use them. Knowing that you must use a hammer when building a house is excellent, but trying to use it for painting a wall is a waste of time. For example, knowing that thought-stopping is a good intervention is great, but trying to use thought-stopping when you should be using avoidance is not effective. Learning the right tool and the right time to use it are both essential.

Noncriminal Support System. We all need help at times. We all need friends to talk to and to interact with, but it is important that your friends support your efforts to improve yourself. When your friends are alcoholics, drug users, or career criminals, they will not encourage you to look honestly at yourself because they can't look honestly at themselves. Sometimes such people (sometimes called "sliding partners") *seem* to support you when they are really helping you stay stuck in old patterns. People who are truly supportive will sometimes tell you things you don't like to hear. Your family, members of your religious group, and offenders who really are changing their lives for the better make the best support people. Even in prison—usually in chapel or in educational and counseling groups—you can find men who are determined to better themselves and who will support your efforts. No matter where or who you are, having someone who understands your situation and is open to giving and receiving feedback is important for change. Don't be like Relapsing Ralph, who was sincere about wanting to change, but didn't change his support system:

My name is Ralph and I'm a sex offender, but I've been in treatment. Before I was arrested, my friends and I really had a thing about doing sexual stuff sort of publicly, trying to show off for each other, I guess. We really didn't have much else in common—the sex thing was our real focus. We went to topless bars together and hired strippers to come to our parties. We even competed with each other in telling our sexual exploits. While we were drinking and partying my friends and I didn't have to think about the rent or the mortgage, the kids getting in trouble at school, the boss coming down hard on us, or any other problem in our lives. We just had a good time.

I gave it all up when I entered treatment. But after three months I was going out of my mind! No drinking, no sex, no friends, and long empty nights. One night I ran into a couple of the guys from our old bunch and they invited me to go drinking with them. I went. It was against everything I learned in treatment, but I was so bored, I wanted to scream. I went right back to all my old habits of drinking and sexually exploiting women. It's taken me a long time to try again to change my life. If I had made some new friends who had a healthier way of being social, I wouldn't have relapsed. I would have been less bored and lonely, if I'd had the support from healthy friends to resist temptation. I've lost so much time!

Determination. You must be convinced that having responsible sexual values benefits you and your potential victims. You must be so convinced that you are *determined* to improve yourself despite all obstacles. If you are honest, willing to change, know the tools to use, but don't feel that the benefits are worth it, you have defeated yourself before you have begun. In earlier S.O.S. workbooks you learned how deviant sexuality affected you as you were growing up and as an adult. You learned that being molested or raped has both short- and long-term consequences to the victim and the perpetrator. All the negative mental, physical, and emotional consequences to you and to your victims aren't worth the brief pleasure or excitement you get from your deviant behavior.

Persistence. Persistence is the ability to continue doing what you know is right and not give up. When you are persistent you are willing to carry on despite setbacks and hard times. Old habits are hard to break. When you have a problem with sexual deviance, it is a lifetime project to gain full control over your behavior. Stopping a bad behavior is easy, just as quitting smoking is easy. Some people quit smoking a hundred times. *Staying* stopped is the hard part. Persistence is the key to leading a sexually healthy life—understanding that bad times and feelings will pass if you just keep using your interventions to change your behavior.

Once you have laid a solid foundation, interventions will work. It is important to understand each of several types of interventions so that you can pick the best one for your problem. Each intervention works best for a certain kind of problem. Each of them has different aims, though all help you stop your deviancy.

Before you can choose an intervention you must understand your patterns of thinking, feeling, and behavior that influence you toward acting out deviantly. These patterns make up your deviant cycle. Once you understand how you act in the various stages of your cycle, you can select an appropriate intervention. The steps of the deviant cycle were discussed in great detail in S.O.S. Two. You may need to go back and review it from time to time. The better you know your deviant cycle, the better you can plan for interventions that will solve your problems as they arise.

Planning for Interventions

When therapists talk about the possibility of reoffending, many men think, "Oh, I don't need to worry about that. I've learned my lesson. I will just stop my bad behavior and be good from now on." If you think like this you are doomed to repeat your crimes. It is like an alcoholic who says, "Oh I'll never drink again," without making plans for *how* he will not drink. A compulsive gambler who says that he will not wager his family's money again, stops gambling,

but doesn't make plans for what to do with his frustration and extra time is doomed to fail.

You must do three things to stop deviant behavior and keep it stopped: *(1) admit the possibility of reoffending; (2) plan how to stop the behavior at the earliest stages of your offense cycle;* and *(3) plan for the time you no longer spend on your deviancy.* For example, an exhibitionist spends hours cruising for victims. The first part of his intervention is to stop cruising. The second part is to figure out what to do with all his extra time. If his intervention does not account for this extra time and the boredom that comes with it, then his intervention will be a failure. This secondary planning is a vital part of a good intervention strategy, one that was missing from Stuck Stan's plan:

My name is Stan, and I'm a cocaine addict. Doing drugs for so many years has cost me my wife, children, job, and self-respect. While using, I committed a rape and went to prison. When I got out I swore I'd go straight. I even wrote it down in a statement, and I gave copies to my minister, my counselor, my lady friend, and my parole officer. I swear I meant it seriously! I really wanted to stand by what I said.

The first months after leaving prison were really bad. I couldn't get a job, no one wanted to hire an ex-con. It wasn't as easy to live with my new lady friend as I thought. My PO put a lot of restrictions on me, and I really resented them. Then I also had all this time dragging on me since I wasn't out hustling for big money to feed my habit. At some point I got really desperate. I was bored and kind of scared—I didn't know what to do with myself, my extra time, and all these wild, scared thoughts and feelings coming up because I had nothing else to do. I didn't have any plan for how to deal with this situation. So I finally had to do something—*anything*—that felt familiar, even if it was a really stupid thing to do: I bought my first hit of coke. It's cost me everything good that I'd worked for.

Types of Interventions

Each of the six types of interventions described below are best suited for a different situation. Some will be covered in detail in later chapters.

Desperate measures are drastic methods you can use if you are close to acting out again. They are simple but effective things that you can do to stop yourself. You must be able to use them instantly. Some examples of this type of intervention include: throwing your glasses out the car window; spilling coffee on yourself; or yelling "Police!" This type of *emergency intervention* is an impulsive and desperate measure that you can use as a *last resort* to give you or your intended victim time to get away.

Environmental controls (also called stimulus control) may be desperate, short-term, or long-term. They focus on changing your environment to reduce your potential for deviant behavior. For example, if you live near a school, you decide (or your Parole Officer asks you) to move. If the adult bookstores tempt you, change the route you drive home. If your deviancy is triggered by the pornography at work, you decide (for your mental health) to ask that the pornography be eliminated or you change jobs, just as Extra-effort Enrico did:

Enrico is my name. I've been working as a custodian in a high school. My probation officer knew I have a problem with exposing myself, but she didn't know I am also tempted to act out around teenagers. So my PO did not tell me to change jobs. In therapy I finally admitted that I was very attracted to some of the female high school students I was around at work. I realized that working around this temptation all the time, it would only be a matter of time until I exposed to a student. I feel really good now because I *did* something to keep myself safe from reoffending: I quit and got a night job in an office building.

Short-term interventions are used in less drastic situations to provide a temporary solution to a problem. For example, if you are angry, you might take a time-out. A time-out is not a lasting solution to anger problems but it is an excellent way to give everyone a chance to calm down. Time-out Tim tried it with some success:

I'm Tim, and I'm a rapist—I've been in prison and went through a mental health treatment program there. Both of my rapes that I was in prison for I did after arguments with women. After getting out of prison, I moved in with Lisa, my new womanfriend. It wasn't that long—maybe a few weeks—before we began having arguments. I was scared that I'd get really mad at her and then try to rape her to show her who's boss, or go out and rape some other woman. But then I remembered what I learned in treatment about dealing with my anger. I started noticing when Lisa and I were raising our voices. Then I'd call a one-hour time-out to give me a chance to cool off, reduce my anger, and think more rationally about what Lisa was saying and feeling. It didn't resolve what we were arguing about, but it saved me from offending again.

Psychological (cognitive) interventions focus on how you think. By identifying unhealthy thoughts, you can change how you think and feel. If you have a problem with anger toward women, for example, you can intervene by looking at your thinking defects. Healthy thinking encourages you to choose healthier ways of interacting with women. Psychological interventions usually take time to work. Thinking Theo managed to learn different ways to relate to women:

My name is Theo. At one time I always felt humiliated by women. Everywhere I went I thought that women were taking advantage of me. When I went out on a date, I paid for dinner. When I got into an argument with a female co-worker, my boss always sided with the woman. I even thought women were using me as the butt of a joke when I would ask a woman out for a date and she would say no. I got angrier and angrier with women until I eventually used my anger to rape a neighbor.

When I joined an anger-management group in prison, I learned that my problem was how *I* was *thinking* about women, *not* what the women were doing. I discovered that I was misinterpreting many women's normal reactions. I also learned that I was using my distorted thinking as a basis for acting strange toward women, which caused them to avoid me. By changing my thinking in big and small ways, I've learned how to develop healthier relationships with some women.

Behavioral interventions focus on what you *do*. If your problem is a behavior—like hitting your wife or cruising for a victim—a behavioral intervention can help you stop. You can use behavioral interventions in either of two ways: to stop unhealthy behaviors, or to start healthy ones. You might start a healthy behavior by rewarding yourself as a positive behavioral intervention when you do the right thing. Changing Chet got rewarded for altering his behavior patterns around food:

My name is Chet and even though I was not fat, I had trouble with overeating: I was using food like some people use drugs. I learned how to look at my patterns of living, and most of my problem came when I was watching TV and food commercials came on. Then I would be bored, go to the kitchen, and load up on chips, peanuts, and pretzels. I learned that I could intervene in my pattern by changing some of my behaviors. I watched more shows on public TV (no commercials). I got a set of second-hand weights to lift so I'd have something else to do during commercials. I kept vegetables on hand to munch on. I felt really rewarded for all these things by losing weight, getting stronger, eating better, and getting compliments. I really started feeling better.

Long-term interventions are used after you are out of crisis. Their main purpose is to help you maintain a healthy life. You can use long-term interventions—journaling and personal maintenance contracts, for example—to change ways of life that contribute to your deviancy. Suppose you have a problem with boredom: when you're very bored, you are more likely to choose to act out deviantly. A long-term intervention might be to decrease your boredom by participating in healthy activities such as joining a bowling league, going back to school, or striving for a better job.

Maintenance means running your life well and keeping crime free. It is a life-long process. Think of it in terms of your health. To keep good health you must regularly eat right, rest, get exercise, and take care of yourself both physically and mentally. Exercising occasionally or having a well-rounded meal once in a while is not good enough. To maintain your mental health you must use your intervention skills often. As with physical fitness training, if you don't use it, you lose it.

Using the right intervention at the right time is the essence of stopping deviant behavior and improving your life. In this workbook you will learn when and how to use several types of interventions. If you are in a treatment program, your therapist can provide additional material.

Chapter 1 Assignments

∽ **Do not write in this workbook** ∽

Note: Some of these assignments will take a considerable amount of time and effort to do well. Take as much time as you need—consider it an investment in your freedom.

1. In your assignment notebook write out the consequences of your deviant behavior on your victims. Consider the following areas: money, health, relationship to parents or spouse, self-esteem, sexuality, trust, drug and alcohol use, depression, sense of safety, and friends.

2. According to this chapter, what is the single most important measure of the success of your treatment? Do you agree or disagree? Why?

3. Define and tell why the following are important in stopping your deviant behavior: internal risk factors, external risk factors, SUD, links, lapse, and relapse.

4. Diagram your deviant cycle. Discuss with your group or therapist how you think, feel, and act during the four stages of your cycle (Build-up, Acting-out, Justification, and Pretend-normal).

5. Define these two terms: Relapse Prevention, Intervention.

6. This chapter lists many conditions that lay the foundation for intervention. Write about how having these foundations would affect the following areas of your life:

Work	Maintaining your offense-free life
Relationships with:	Finances
your wife	Leisure time
your children	Home life
your parents	Sexuality

7. Why must you make detailed plans in order not to reoffend?

8. Think about the amount of time you have spent in your life on your deviant sexual behavior. Include time spent planning, fantasizing, cruising, using pornography, thinking angry thoughts, being depressed, using drugs and alcohol, etc. Add all this time up. How many total hours have you spent on deviant behavior? How many hours per day? Week? Month? Year?

9. Why must you plan for the time you do NOT spend on your deviancy?

10. Give one example for each item of a time in your life when you could have used the following interventions: desperate measures, short-term interventions, environmental controls, psychological (cognitive) interventions, behavioral interventions, and long-term interventions.

Review your answers to these assignments with your therapist and your group. If you are working on your own, share your answers with a friend or person you trust.

2.
Desperate Measures:
Planning Emergency Escapes from
My Offending Behaviors

"A RECOVERING OFFENDER PLANS TO ESCAPE **before**, not after, a crime."

If You Are on the Verge of Reoffending ...

It is a sad fact, but you might commit another sexual crime. If you do, it is likely to happen when your life seems meaningless or is filled with greed. When you are in either of these states you feel desperate.

Think about it: *sooner or later, you will be as desperate as you were before committing your last crime.* What will you do then?

When you feel desperate you will be closer to reoffending. You must be prepared to intervene in your deviant cycle right up to the last second. Anything you can do to put time between yourself and a new crime gives you greater control over yourself. A desperate behavior which stops you for an extra half-hour might make the difference between a life in prison and a life of freedom. You have to think rationally about your emergency escape plans *before* you need them. If you do not think about them now while your mind is clear, you will have a much harder time later when you are not thinking as clearly.

To be prepared for an emergency intervention, you must plan when you are calm and reasonable and your motivation is high. Even if you are working hard on yourself now, later you are likely to forget what you have learned, return to denial, and say, "To hell with it all." Because of this possibility, you must learn what signs show you are close to committing an offense. Before you are ready to make an emergency escape, you must take several steps; the first step is to *establish your* **Destruction Warning Line**.

Your Destruction Warning (DeW) Line

The last border you step over before you destroy yourself and your victim with a new offense is your *Destruction Warning (DeW) Line*. The DeW Line is your list of *last behaviors*, the deviant things you do just before you reoffend. It is true that if you *decide* to reoffend you will. *But you don't have to. If you are really committed to **not acting out**, you won't.* The DeW Line is a little bit of insurance against reoffending. Consider Lapsing Larry's case:

My name is Larry. I'm a rapist. I've got a rap sheet as long as your arm, including fights, robberies, and rape. In prison I was in a sex-offender treatment program and spent *four years* turning my life around. I did everything they asked me to, including this DeW Line thing. For *two years* after I got out of treatment and out of prison I did pretty well in the community. By the third year me and my wife Margaret were having problems with money and with our marriage. I went back into my old, not-too-bright ways of living. I wouldn't talk to Margaret or anybody else for that matter, came home as late as possible or not at all, and started drinking beer. I really didn't know how far I had slid.

One day last fall I was walking on the beach. I had my jack-knife in my jacket. I saw a young woman walking alone and slowly caught up with her. I came up behind her and got my jackknife out. It's weird, but right then I remembered my DeW Line from treatment. I knew I was on that line and my future freedom was on that line. If I took one more step toward her I'd be across the line. I stopped, apologized for scaring the young woman, and ran off. I knew then that I was in serious trouble: if I didn't get help I would rape again.

You can stop yourself from reoffending by intervening at any point in your deviant cycle, but it gets harder and harder the more deeply you enter your cycle and the closer you get to the line. Think in advance about the details of this line. In order for you to be able to intervene successfully, you need to *know* when you are on the edge of reoffending. Think about mental, emotional, physical, and environmental signs, like the examples listed below, that show you are near a reoffense.

Mental signs: depression, hatred, resentment, extreme despair, or giving up; fantasizing about having sex with a woman who is innocently talking to you; thinking about equipment you might need to kidnap a victim; or imagining if you work it right, you could seduce *that* boy.

Physical signs: not washing or shaving, feeling sick, not sleeping, masturbating several times a day, or feeling tense all the time.

Environmental signs: spending time in places that you know are dangerous for you—a bar, a boys' club, places where prostitutes hang out, or at the home of a friend who has children.

Get in the habit of asking yourself, "On a scale from 1 to 10, *how close am I to reoffending?*" When you ask, "*Am I* close to reoffending?" the easy answer ("No") is no good. A 1-to-10 judgment about how close you are makes you think, "Well, I guess I'm about at 6. That is over halfway to a reoffense." The more judgment you use about your situation, the less likely you will decide to reoffend.

To establish your DeW Line you need to define a set of *behavioral warning flags*—concrete behaviors that show you are in danger. When you ask yourself if you have or have not done them, you must be able to say yes or no. You must set these behavioral flags for any area you feel has been a problem, including:

using alcohol	eating
yelling	going into taverns and bars
isolating yourself	seeing movies
driving	walking
being around women or children	following a potential victim
masturbating	drinking and trying to pick up a woman
using pornography	agreeing to babysit
having idle time	picking up a hitch-hiker
hanging out with drug friends	

Divide a piece of paper in half vertically. On the left, list 10 *early* warning signs (the first behavior that shows you have a problem). Your *early* warning signs might be: stepping into an adult bookstore, buying a copy of *Penthouse* or *True Detective*, or taking second looks at the centerfolds at work. On the right, list 10 DeW Line signs (your *last* behavior before you self-destruct by reoffending). Your *DeW Line signs* might be: buying a bondage magazine, getting some handcuffs, masturbating in your car, or showing pornography to a child. All your last and most dangerous behaviors before reoffending make up your DeW Line. Once you have figured yours out, write it down and post it where you can see and read it every day. Later, if you find yourself crossing this line, you will know that you need to take desperate measures. Consider Loser Leon's and DeW Line Denny's cases:

I'm Leon and I've been a cocaine addict and sex offender. I was in a residential treatment program and got chemically clean and sexually controlled. I did really well in the program and thought I'd never start using again. I just knew it so strong that when I got out of the program I said to myself, "There's no need to keep doing all that garbage. It's unnecessary. I'm going to do okay on my own." And I did fine for about a year. But then I started hanging out with my old drug buddies. A few months later I got desperate, lapsed, and I felt so bad about lapsing, I went on a cocaine run. I lost my sobriety, my wife, my job, and my freedom all at the same time.

Denny is my name. I've been addicted to methamphetamines. I was in treatment in the same program as "Leon." We helped each other in there sometimes, gave each other support. I did pretty well. While in therapy I couldn't imagine returning to my old ways, just like Leon. After I left, I lost track of him. But I said to myself, "just in case." So, I made up a DeW Line for myself that included: seeing an illegal drug, being around when someone was buying drugs, and calling to set up a drug deal. I did okay in the community for months. Then I started seeing some old friends and enjoyed it. About a month ago I was with a friend who stopped to make a drug deal. I wasn't using or buying right then, but I remembered my DeW Line. I had to ask myself if I was at risk to use again. In all honesty, I had to say yes. I found out that I had gotten very loose about my decision not to use drugs. My friends noticed and felt that I wouldn't mind if they used around me. I knew that I was on the edge of trouble and went back to my support group. That's where I heard about Leon not making it.

As you think about your DeW Line consider what your flags would be in the following areas:

Spotting a Victim. What are the signs that say to you, "I have crossed the line between being in the same area as a potential victim and *spotting* a victim"? Spotting a potential victim is easy and common. If you are a rapist, you notice women. You notice them walking alone, leaving their cars, driving, and in bars. In fact, wherever you and women are, there are potential victims. If you are a child molester, you notice children. You notice them playing, walking home from school, in groups, in parks, riding their bikes, almost everywhere.

Approaching a Potential Victim. What thoughts, feelings, and actions show that you are approaching a victim? When you are thinking clearly, you know when to say, "I'm in the wrong place, at the wrong time, with the wrong person." Think about what step says that you are a danger to yourself or your victim. This step may be talking to a woman in a bar, stopping a child on the street, watching a boy play video games, or even smiling at someone. *You must decide what your dangerous line is.*

Beginning to Set Up a Victim. Ask yourself, "At what point does my dangerous set-up behavior start?" If children are your victims, is your DeW Line when you invite them into your house? When you start photographing them? If adults are your victims, is your DeW Line when you walk near a stranger? Pick up a hitch-hiker? Isolate a woman at a bar? Decide now so you will recognize it later.

Making Decisions to Weaken Your Resistance. What kinds of things do you do to lower your resistance to a crime? Just before you commit a crime you do something to make it easier. Do you do a lesser crime first (for example, before you rape a stranger in her home, you steal from a prostitute on the street)? Do you use alcohol or drugs to help you "get in the mood" to do a crime? Do you watch a live sex show to make it easier to force someone to have sex? Do you buy a gun or a knife so you will feel more confident?

Desperate Measures

Once you establish your DeW Line you are ready to plan for emergency interventions. Whatever intervention you plan to use just before a crime must be desperate. It must be something you can use automatically and instantly. Consider Escaping Evan's case:

My name is Evan and I'm a rapist. I was in therapy in 1980, got out, changed my life, and remarried. In 1987 I was having trouble in my marriage, began drinking, and lost my job. Over a few weeks I was drinking more and more and I started cruising for victims. In the back of my mind there was a little voice, saying, *"Evan, you're getting into deep trouble here."* I only figured out how deep I was in the night I stopped in front of a mini-market near closing time to watch a female cashier. I had all my rape equipment with me: a knife, a roll of duct tape, and the intent to rape.

I knew in some part of my mind that I was about to harm myself and my wife, as well as my intended victim. Part of my mind said, *"Who cares, I've ruined everything already,"* while another part of me said, ***"Please, not again."***

Standing on that corner waiting for the store to close and the cashier to be alone, I felt like I was drowning, so I made one huge effort to save myself with my emergency plan. I cut myself with the knife, then threw it away. The wound wasn't deep, but it hurt. I got myself to the hospital emergency room and told the doctor who sewed me up that I was afraid I would do something terrible. The doctor sent me to the hospital social worker. After waiting, talking, and getting more sober, my impulse to rape died down temporarily. Later I made an emergency phone call to my old therapist who said I could see him the next day. I felt really relieved.

For Evan, this emergency plan worked. It cost him less in time, money, and personal pain than trying to deal with the consequences of a reoffense.

Elements of an Emergency Plan

What do you plan to do when you get to your DeW Line? First, decide on actions that will force you to put *any amount of time* between you and a reoffense. Free your mind so you can think about novel solutions and interventions. Consider what thoughts will be compelling or what behaviors will distract your atten-

tion from your crime. *Even an extra moment is helpful.* Second, decide what your basic backup plans will be.

Think of everything you could conceivably do to stop yourself. Write down 25 ideas; they do not all have to be reasonable at this stage. The list below is made up of desperate measures sex offenders like you have used.

- A nearsighted rapist threw away his glasses while following a woman so he couldn't see her.
- A child molester close to acting out with his daughter spilled hot coffee on his lap. He then had to leave the room and change.
- An exhibitionist threw his car keys down a storm grate to immobilize his escape vehicle, forcing him to postpone his deviant behavior.
- A child molester went and sat in the police station.
- A rapist broke a window in a store and waited for the police.
- A peeper yelled, "HELP" loudly, near a house where he was spying.
- A pedophile started cursing and scared his victim off.

Some of these examples may seem drastic or silly. But it is better to be embarrassed, picked up for breaking a window, or even hurt than it is to commit another sexual offense. Glass can be replaced, lives cannot. These examples are not solutions; they are time-catchers that give you a few moments more to work with. Once you have given yourself some time, you must use your regular interventions. Decide who you will call, where you will go, which of the regular interventions you will use.

No matter how many crimes you have committed in the past, you are still not lost. If you relapse and commit another offense, you will have a price to pay but you can still stop yourself from committing more crimes in the future. Don't give up—don't let the *Abstinence Violation Effect* get you. Giving up and committing a crime is always worse than holding on to your vows, no matter how painful it may be.

Chapter 2 Assignments

⚭ Do not write in this workbook ⚭

11. Share with your group (or your friend if working alone) what it felt like when you were absolutely desperate for four of the following: money, respect, security, love, escape, and transportation. For each area write out examples of good ways and bad ways you handled those feelings.

12. Before your last crime did you struggle with yourself—did one part of your mind say "yes" and another say "no"? Write down the thoughts you had about the two sides of your struggle. How long did this struggle last?

13. Define the Destruction Warning Line.

14. Write out your Destruction Warning signs. What thoughts, feelings, physical sensations, environments, and behaviors would be involved if you were about to commit another crime? Be very specific: identify five signs for each area.

15. Ask yourself once a day for the next 3 months, "On a 1-10 scale how close to reoffending am I?" Write down these answers in your notebook and on a calendar. (If your answer is always 1, meaning not at all, you haven't really looked at yourself.)

16. Write down early warning signs and DeW Line signs for the following areas:

alcohol use	driving	masturbation
eating	movies	approaching a victim
yelling	women	pornography
drug friends	walking	isolating
children	idle time	taverns and bars
spotting a victim	setting up a victim	

17. Write 25 ideas you could use to put time between yourself and another victim. Let your mind run wild, allow yourself a few far-out ideas. Share them with your group or friend.

18. Define the Abstinence Violation Effect. How has it affected you in the past?

Review your answers to these assignments with your therapist and your group. If you are working on your own, share your answers with a friend or person you trust.

3.

Controlling My Environment

IF YOU ARE A CONVICTED SEX OFFENDER, your behavior in the community will probably be restricted with special conditions set by the court or your probation/parole officer. For example, conditions of probation or parole might include not using alcohol or drugs, attending Alcoholics Anonymous (AA) or Narcotics Anonymous (NA) meetings, or not having contact with a minor.

These conditions are *environmental controls* and their purpose is to help you avoid risk factors. Accepting your need for these controls gives you another bit of insurance against reoffending and reassures the community. Many offenders resent these controls, but their actions have shown they need them. When you are sincere about wanting to change your life, you accept the safety that environmental controls provide and participate by setting additional limits for yourself.

Stimulus Control

The primary purpose of environmental controls is to help you limit your environment so it contains few triggers for your deviant thoughts, feelings, and behaviors. Environmental controls help you avoid high-risk factors. To prevent yourself from acting out, remove potential problems from your environment. This kind of stimulus control requires assertive problem-solving behavior; other methods, like avoidance and escape (Chapters Four and Five), require planning.

One way to have some control of your life is by cooperating with your probation or parole officer (PO) and/or therapist and letting them know what additional controls you need to keep yourself and your potential victims safe. Whether these controls are formal (as in parole conditions), or informal (as in an agreement),

you can decrease your risk of reoffending by preparing and following your environmental control plan. Three common sets of controls include: *(1) general environmental controls* involving potential problem areas common to many sexual offenders (most could apply to you); *(2) rapist-specific environmental controls*, or *(3) child molester-specific environmental controls* may apply to you depending on your offense pattern.

General Controls

- Successfully enroll in, participate in, and complete an approved sex-offender treatment program in the community.
- Give your PO search and seizure privileges for drugs and pornography.
- Do not use alcohol.
- Do not use illicit drugs or any other drugs, unless prescribed by a doctor.
- Submit to urinalysis upon request (to check for drug and alcohol use).
- Take Antabuse under supervision.
- Maintain use of prescribed medications (i.e. antidepressants).
- Do not go to bars, taverns, or places where alcoholic beverages are served.
- Do not associate with alcohol and drug users.
- Do not go to topless bars, adult bookstores, X-rated movie theaters, massage parlors, or other places that promote prostitution, adult sex shows, etc.
- Agree to polygraph or physiological assessment at the request of your therapist or PO.
- Attend all meetings with your PO.
- Attend AA or NA meetings weekly.
- Attend an alcohol and/or drug abuse treatment program.
- Maintain a driving log including the time, route driven, and miles.
- Do not possess a weapon.

- Do not use or possess pornography or erotica (*Playboy, Gent, Hustler,* etc.).
- Do not associate with ex-felons, other than those offenders who are currently in treatment with you and are approved by your PO and/or therapist.
- Do not have any contact with males or females under the age of 18 at work or in social situations unless accompanied by an approved responsible adult who is aware of your sexual deviancy.
- Live in a residence approved by your PO and/or therapist.
- Obey any curfew set by your PO and/or therapist.
- Do not watch TV, videos, or movies that glorify your pattern of offending.
- Maintain full-time school and/or employment.
- Have no contact with victim(s) unless approved by your PO, therapist, victim's therapist, and victim (or victim's parents).
- Attend a once-a-week verifiable social activity (club, church, etc.).
- Keep a log of daily activities.
- Keep a written budget of money earned and spent.

Rapist-specific Controls

- Do not drive alone at night or at key times when you would offend.
- Do not drive aimlessly without a specific purpose or destination.
- Do not pick up hitch-hikers.
- Do not drive alone with a single female or single vulnerable male.

- Do not go to or from work on streets where prostitutes hang out.
- Do not possess any of the items that you have used for past rapes, like tape, knives, rope, wire, etc.

Child Molester-specific Controls

- Do not be in the presence of children unless in the company of a responsible adult who is aware of your deviancy.
- Do not possess a camera.
- Do not keep catalogs containing illustrations of children's clothing.
- Do not go to parks, schools, playgrounds, malls, arcades, or other places where children congregate.
- Do not live near schools, parks, or playgrounds.
- Live in an adult-oriented apartment complex or in a neighborhood that is largely adult.
- Do not hold any job that involves contact with children.
- Do not associate or have contact with persons under the age of 18.
- Do not socialize with women or men who have children.

This list is far more extensive than those used by most criminal justice agencies. Consider the items on the list and see which you feel apply to your situation. Choose to use these controls for your protection as well as the protection of the community. They will help you learn new habits to keep yourself offense-free.

Chapter 3 Assignments

 Do not write in this workbook

19. Review the list of environmental controls above. Write down each control that you think applies to you. Add at least three others that apply specifically to you and are important for you to follow.

20. List why you think each of these controls is important. What risk situations do you think they could help you avoid?

21. USE THESE CONTROLS!

Review your answers to these assignments with your therapist and your group. If you are working on your own, share your answers with a friend or person you trust.

4.

Avoidance Strategies

YOU ACT (OR REACT) WHEN YOU MEET A TRIGGER for deviant behavior. When a trigger is very strong you respond quickly. For example, choosing to watch an X-rated movie will rapidly encourage you to masturbate. If you are a child molester, choosing to be alone with a child fuels your deviant fantasies. If you are a rapist, picking up a hitch-hiker is a trigger for rape. Avoiding high-risk situations—making sure you do not get involved in them—is the first and best intervention.

What Is Avoidance?

Because avoidance is so easy to understand, it is often the first intervention discussed in treatment. Basically, you should avoid any situation, event, person, object, or place strongly associated with your offenses. If you cannot totally avoid these triggers, minimize the amount of time you are exposed to them. When you avoid factors that you might use to allow yourself to reoffend, you will not act out again. This idea is simple to understand and use.

To use avoidance strategies, you must think about your offense patterns and plan ahead. Review your past offenses. Figure out what triggers for sexual deviance were present before you acted out. Focus on both little and big triggers. A little trigger might be standing in the mini-market looking at the pornographic magazines. A big trigger might be going to a nude beach. It is better to identify too many triggers than too few, even if some seem far-fetched. The more triggers you understand, the safer you will be. In this kind of planning, you're using the negative parts of your past to help you create a positive future.

Triggers you might find from the past may include: for an alcoholic, bars, taverns, liquor stores, or listen-ing to sad music; for a rapist, aimless driving, streets where hitch-hikers were found, places where prostitutes hang out, or pornography; for a child molester, parks, malls, video arcades, babysitting, or having your daughter's friends visit.

When Do I Use Avoidance?

You can use avoidance in two different ways. First, you can use it to *plan* what triggers you need to avoid. Being invited to a social event where children will be present is a classic example of when you can apply this type of avoidance, as Dodger Dan did:

My name is Dan, and I molested a child five years ago and went to prison for four years. I've been out of prison for five months. As part of my sex-offender treatment since I've been out, I've been putting together a group of adult friends and working on how to be social with adults. Last week, a member of my square dance club invited me to a potluck dinner he was having for the club. Jack asked me to bring a dessert since there would be a lot of hungry kids there. It was a real problem for me to know what to do: if I turned down the invitation, it might look like I was being unfriendly; then again, I just can't be around kids and not do weird sexual things in my head with it. I told Jack that I'd have to let him know, I might have a conflict. Then I remembered the strategy we were learning in my offender group about avoidance. So I avoided this risky social situation by telling Jack that I really appreciated the invitation, but I just couldn't make it. I knew I might sit around the night of the potluck stewing about how everyone else was having a good time except me, so I called up my friend Burt and we went out for pizza and had an okay time.

Avoidance also can be used as a coping strategy when you unexpectedly find yourself facing a high-risk factor. Focused Frank used this second type of avoidance when he was caught in line at a supermarket:

My name is Frank and I molested kids. But I've learned a lot about staying away from kids and out of trouble since I was in treatment. Like last Wednesday night, as usual, I went to the supermarket for groceries. I checked it out by watching every night for a week, and Wednesday is the night when kids usually aren't in the store. I was in line with a shopping cart full of food, and as the cashier started ringing me up, this woman with two kids got in line behind me. Not only that, but the little girl was the same age as my last victim. First I thought, "Oh God, lady, stay away from me!" Then I thought, "Frankie, it's not her job, *you* gotta stay away from them! What the hell am I gonna do now?" This was my neighborhood store, so I didn't want to make a scene by leaving without the food and without paying or explaining or *something.* So I thought fast and decided I would be okay if I avoided looking at or talking to those children. But then I thought, "Well, Frankie boy, you've got to start thinking about something else, too, or you're gonna be headed for trouble!" So I started talking to the cashier—she's a nice lady about 50, likes to feed the birds. So we talked about birds while she finished ringing up my stuff. We just kept talking and I stopped wondering about those kids behind me. She bagged my order and I left. I usually read the bulletin board on my way out, but that night I *boogied*—I didn't want to be around when the kids came out. I felt like I did real good at staying away from trouble.

In this case Frank had tried to avoid the high-risk factor by shopping on a low-risk night. But since he was in line and his groceries were being checked, he decided not to just abandon the cart and leave the store (an escape strategy). Instead, Frank extended his avoidance strategy in two ways: first, by choosing not to look at or interact with the children; and second, by taking his mind off them through engaging the cashier in conversation.

Avoidance works on a simple principle: if you avoid people, places, things, situations, or events that are triggers in your offense, you will not reoffend.

Many men think avoidance is too simple or too much trouble, and they stop using it. Sometimes they reason that since they haven't acted out in several months, avoiding triggers and risk situations is no longer necessary. But once you have a trigger or risk factor you will always have it. You will always be responsive to triggers. The *intensity* of your response may decrease, but the risk is always there. If you don't continue to use avoidance, you may start getting closer to a relapse, as Overconfident Otis discovered:

My name is Otis, and I'm an exhibitionist—I flash my penis at women. At one point I could not drive down a road used by joggers without stopping and looking for a victim. In therapy, I learned to avoid roads joggers used. Five months ago, I was late to work and took an old shortcut that was popular with joggers. No problem. I wasn't even *thinking* about looking for a victim or flashing—all I could think about was getting to work on time. After trying it a few more times without needing to stop, I was feeling pretty comfortable and confident. I decided that I had overcome my problem and I'd be safe wherever I went. With this sense of security, I started *really enjoying* driving past all those joggers. In fact, occasionally I stopped so I could enjoy watching them. Over a period of four months I watched the joggers and thought I was doing okay— what a lie *that* was! Then I began to fantasize about flashing again. Two weeks ago, after my wife, Jackie, and I had an argument, I headed straight for the joggers' lane, found a victim, and flashed. I'm back in therapy while I'm waiting for my sentencing.

Because Otis got comfortable, dismissed a trigger, and put himself into a high-risk situation, he acted out again. Once you have a trigger, you will always have a trigger. Making avoidance a lifetime habit will help you not to reoffend.

Chapter 4 Assignments

22. Where did Otis first go wrong? Write down some thinking defects he might have used to give himself permission to lapse and take the next step toward relapse.

23. While thinking about avoidance as a strategy, review your past offenses. Write down the risk factors or triggers that were present before you acted out. Focus on both little and big triggers. (Remember, it is better to identify too many triggers than not enough. The more triggers you know you must avoid, the safer you will be.)

24. Now think about the plans you will make to avoid your risk situations. Write them out and share them with your group or a friend, if you are working alone. *USE THESE PLANS!*

25. Write down three situations you can think of where avoidance is *not* the best strategy.

Review your answers to these assignments with your therapist and your group. If you are working on your own, share your answers with a friend or person you trust.

5.

Escape Strategies

USING AVOIDANCE STRATEGIES WILL PREVENT YOU from putting yourself into high-risk situations. But occasionally you will unexpectedly find yourself in the middle of one. This is when *escape strategies* are important. For example, you visit a friend and company drops in unannounced. One of the visitors is just like your victim. Your friend needs to run down to the corner store for coffee and asks you to stay and entertain his guests. You could not have avoided this situation in advance, but you can *escape* from it. To escape means "to leave." If your avoidance strategies have not worked, escape is the next intervention to use. Even when you cannot avoid a risky situation, you can always escape from it.

Frank's situation in the supermarket in the last chapter is a good example. He planned his shopping trip for a time when children were not likely to be present (avoidance). If Frank had noticed the children when he entered the store, he could have escaped from the risk situation by leaving and coming back later. When you escape from risk situations, you will not reoffend.

What Is An Escape Strategy?

An escape strategy is an intervention that gets you out of a high-risk situation. It is used as a backup to avoidance. If you were in the path of a semitractor-trailer (a dangerous situation), you would leave as quickly as possible. When you are in a situation that is dangerous to maintaining your offense-free life, you have to escape. Planning escapes is like having fire drills—they work best when you make plans in advance.

As an intervention, escape requires that you act quickly. The longer you put off escaping, the more dif-

ficult it becomes. If you were hanging off the edge of a cliff, the longer you hung, the weaker you would be, and the harder it would be to climb to safety. The longer you put off escaping, the closer you come to lapsing or relapsing, just like Slowpoke Steve:

My name is Steve, and I've been in prison for molesting children and raping both children and women. In my treatment program, I learned about escape strategies and wrote a list of all my risk situations. Dating women who drink and use drugs, accepting a drink, and being alone with young girls are all dangerous for me.

A couple of months ago I went with a friend to a party. I *knew* there would be people drinking and using drugs, but I told myself that I had been so good, and I was so bored, that I deserved a little fun. Besides, it had been a while since I had had any problem with my behavior.

At the party I met a young woman, Jennifer. She giggled and whispered in my ear that she was only 16, but she was trying to pass for 18 so she could have some beer. I *knew* I shouldn't be around her, and my mental alarm was ringing like crazy, but I wasn't listening. Jennifer was lovely, sweet, charming, and I told myself she was quite mature for her age. I was already feeling sexually aroused when she asked me to get beer for us. I knew this was a *very* high-risk situation and I should use my escape strategy: I could make my excuses, find Ben, and leave. "Aw, c'mon," I told myself. "You're not doing anything bad. You've worked so hard—You can handle this. One beer won't hurt."

It was noisy in the livingroom, so I went into a side room—a guest room—with Jennifer. We talked, one beer led to another, and there was no place to sit except on the bed. I was feeling more and more turned on and I told myself, "She's really a fox. I know just what she wants." I told her we were going for a walk where we could be alone and *really* get to know each other, and I grabbed her arm. She knew that I was talking about sex and tried to pull her arm away. She said, "Look, Steve, you're nice and everything, but I don't want to leave the party. Besides, I'm not interested in sex right now." By this time I was on my third beer, and I decided that she was just flirting with me, teasing me. Looking back now, I understand that *my* wrong thinking was the problem—not what she was doing. I was reaching for the front of her blouse—I was so mad I wanted to rip it right off her—just as Jennifer's older sister walked into the room wanting to know what was going on. I was so angry! I thought, "She was just playing with me. Damn, if that sister hadn't walked in, I could have had a *good* time making her give in." Jennifer's sister made kind of a scene, but fortunately, Ben got me out of the apartment before I did anything else stupid.

Look at Steve's behavior. He broke his treatment contract by drinking the first beer, kept himself in a high-risk situation by not leaving the party when he first started feeling attracted to a young girl, violated his parole by furnishing alcohol to a minor, lapsed by choosing to be in a room alone with her, lied to himself all along to keep his deviant behavior going, and came within a hair of raping a 16-year-old. *This* time, it was only luck that had kept Steve from reoffending and going back to prison. But if he had escaped early, he would not have come so close to reoffending.

What Am I Escaping?

Some of your risk situations are similar to those of other sex offenders, and some are very different. The list below describes a few examples of common risk situations appropriate for escape strategies.

1. You go out for a walk and see a new adult book store.
2. You go to a party and someone offers you a beer.
3. You have finished dinner at a truck stop and as you leave, a hitch-hiker asks for a ride.
4. You are walking in the woods and you see a group of teenage girls.

5. While you are riding on a bus a group of children get on and one takes the empty seat next to you.
6. You bump into some old friends who invite you over to their house where they offer you drugs.
7. You go to a bachelor party where the host puts on an X-rated movie.
8. A friend asks you to sit with her five-year-old while she puts more money in the parking meter.

By now, you should begin to get a sense of when to use escape strategies. The exercises below will help you understand when you might need to use one.

Take time right now to think about the eight high-risk situations above. Think about what you would do or say as your escape strategy for each one.

Now, compare your answers with the list of possible answers below.

How I Could Escape

1. Turn and walk away from the adult book stores. Take a different street one or two blocks over to get where you are going. Remind yourself that you are at risk.
2. Say, "No thanks." Leave the party. Excuse yourself and talk with someone else if you are unable to leave.
3. Say, "No." Tell the hitch-hiker you don't give rides. Tell the hitch-hiker you are just going a few blocks. Tell the hitch-hiker it's not your car and you can't give anyone a ride. Whatever you do, do not get into a discussion. Get into your car or truck and lock the doors.
4. Turn around and walk back the way you came. Do not go past the girls. Do not stop to talk with them. Do not walk in the same direction they are walking in.

5. Stand up, and get off at the next stop after the kids get on. Avoid looking at or talking with the kids until you can get off. Take another bus.

6. Tell the person you don't get high. Immediately tell the person you need to leave.

7. Tell the others that you don't like "porno flicks." Get up and go into the kitchen and do the dishes. Leave the party.

8. Tell your friend you will not watch the child. Offer to go out to the car and put more money in the meter for her. Tell her you feel uncomfortable being alone with children, but you could all walk to the car together.

Discuss these strategies in your treatment group, with your therapist, or with your friend.

Chapter 5 Assignments

Do not write in this workbook

26. How does *escape* differ from *avoidance*? When should you use each?

27. List 20 situations you might get into where you need an escape strategy. Note: These are often very different from situations you avoid.

28. For each situation you listed in Assignment #25, write out a reasonable escape plan. Then read these plans every day and use them when necessary.

Review your answers to these assignments with your therapist and your group. If you are working on your own, share your answers with a friend or person you trust.

6.
Stopping My Deviant Thoughts

YOU *THINK* BOTH BEFORE AND AFTER your deviant behavior. One way of stopping your deviant behavior or keeping it from recurring is to change how you think. What you think before your deviant behavior gives you permission to engage in the behavior. What you think after your deviant behavior strengthens your pattern and makes it easier for you to do it again.

Thought-stopping is an effective intervention you can use to change your thinking. You can use it anytime and any place. It does not require any special skills.

Thought-stopping has four steps: (1) awareness of thought, (2) identifying undesirable thoughts, (3) stopping undesirable thoughts, and (4) replacing undesirable thoughts with healthy thoughts.

Step One: Becoming Aware of Thoughts

Most of the time your thoughts are automatic and you don't pay attention to them. They come and go continually without your control. Learning to notice what is going on in your mind is the first step to stopping the thoughts you use to encourage your deviant behavior.

Consider what you would have to do to stop smoking, swearing, biting your nails, or using alcohol. For example, if you tried to stop swearing, first you had to pay attention to what swear words you said. Then you had to notice when you were *about* to swear. When you failed and said the swear words, you tried to catch yourself sooner. As you paid more attention, your skill increased. When you were aware enough, you began succeeding. With no awareness, there is no change.

Stopping thoughts requires you first to pay attention to your thoughts, and second, to notice the feelings and behaviors that follow your thoughts. Wake-up Wes's case history illustrates the first step:

My name is Wes, and I've been molesting children since I was 15. Now that I'm 38, I really want to turn my life around, so I'm now in a treatment program for sex offenders. I've got some bad habits I need to change. I think about children a lot. I remember exciting times I've had with children, like meeting new kids, getting to know them, and being sexual with them.

I know I need to change. I'm really tired of letting my deviancy run my life. Before I was in treatment I was scared all the time that one of the kids I was sexual with would report me. Now I also know that being sexual with kids hurts them for a long time, and I don't want to do that any more. To help me change my thinking, my therapist asked me to keep a "thought log," where I write down the time, place, and intensity of every thought I have about kids. Writing it all down takes a lot of time, and I discovered that I think about children five or six times an hour. I use these thoughts to create sexual fantasies about the children. Sometimes my thoughts about children were just short "snapshots," and sometimes they were long and complicated. In keeping my log, I realized that watching TV, reading certain books, looking at some magazines and catalogs, thinking about the past, and being near children all encouraged me to think about kids.

I have a lot more thoughts about children than I ever imagined. Thoughts of kids interrupt all of my activities. I discovered that I was looking for ways to increase my fantasies about kids because I was enjoying them. For years I've been thinking constantly about children at any time of day, and no matter what else I was doing.

Step Two: Identifying Undesirable Thoughts

After you have increased your awareness of your thoughts, you must begin to identify when you engage in *undesirable* thoughts. You must be specific about which thoughts are inappropriate. It is hard to succeed when your goal is too broad: for example, "to not think bad thoughts." It is easier to succeed when you intervene with specific thoughts or types of thoughts. For example, you might want to intervene in certain kinds of angry thoughts, sexual thoughts, or depressing thoughts.

Suppose your goal is to stop treating women as sexual objects or playthings. First, become aware of your thoughts about women. Second, you identify any thoughts or ideas that feed your destructive attitude and behavior. You might decide that thoughts relating to a woman as sexual parts (as in the expression, "tits and ass") are wrong. Third, you make a list of all the wrong thoughts you can think of. Then you can begin to stop yourself as the identified thoughts come into your mind.

Step Three: Stopping Undesirable Thoughts

Once you have identified your inappropriate thoughts, you can stop or alter them. Your intent is to *stop the undesirable thought as early as possible.* Eventually, you'll catch yourself just as you start thinking the undesirable thought. Then you can use positive "self-talk" techniques to help yourself disengage from the undesirable thought process. Wes, the child molester, was determined to stop his deviant thoughts:

> I kept writing out the thoughts I usually had about children: "He's cute"; "He looks sad"; "He reminds me of ..."; "Wouldn't it be fun if I did _____ with him"; etc.
>
> Next, I started to spot it each time I had a flash or a thought about children. My increased awareness helped me catch my inappropriate thoughts just as they began. It has put me more in control: now I'm on the offensive and no longer at the mercy of my deviant thoughts. Now I can *do* something about my undesirable thoughts.

When you catch yourself beginning to have an undesirable thought, you must take immediate action to stop it. One way of doing this is to yell "STOP!" or "NO!" the moment you recognize the undesirable thought. It works best when you say it out loud, but it also works if you stop what you're doing for a moment and say it in your mind. You probably will need to do both. Practicing this technique by saying "STOP!" or "NO!" aloud at first will make this intervention more effective. If you only try to say "NO!" in your head, you may forget to say it. Once you have stopped an unhealthy or wrong thought, you need to replace it a positive, healthy thought.

Step Four: Replacing Undesirable Thoughts

When you stop an undesirable thought, your mind will not stay empty: you must start a healthy thought to replace it, either by switching your thoughts to a new topic, or by using self-talk that promotes self-esteem, as Wes learned to do:

> Last Monday I caught myself thinking about having sex with a boy I had seen. I quickly yelled, "Wes, NO!" And then I switched to my good self-talk. I told myself, "Wanting to have sex with that boy is dangerous. He does not want to have sex with me. I do not want to hurt any more children. I am doing well in my treatment and making progress. I am proud that I can catch these thoughts and stop them right away. When I use these techniques they work for me and I feel confident I can control my behavior." So I was able to turn my mind from my wrong thoughts about deviant sex to positive thoughts about my progress.

The method you use to replace your unhealthy thoughts will depend on what you are doing at the time. If you are operating a piece of machinery or involved in another task requiring attention, the best thing to do is to focus intensely on what is in front of you. Pulling your attention away from your task would not be safe. If you are doing something requiring less concentration (like watching TV), you can focus on rational, positive thoughts as Wes did:

So, I countered my undesirable thoughts that time. Then, later, I went to my construction site, where I work as a carpenter. Once again, I noticed my deviant thoughts coming into my mind. I said inside my mind, "STOP!" Then I worked hard to focus on the tricky little cabinet joint I was trying to get just right. I concentrated on what my next step in shaping the joint would be and on doing the best job I could. When my mind wandered, I reminded myself, "Wes, you're a good carpenter and you want to be known for quality work." So I managed to work both on controlling my thoughts and on my carpentry skills.

Since he's been practicing thought-stopping, Wes has discovered that his undesirable thoughts come back less often. This intervention has paid off for him: Wes knows he is not helpless and he is not a slave to his undesirable thoughts. He feels better about himself, as does Stopper Stuart:

My name is Stuart, I'm 28 years old, married with two children. I began raping at age 16, and have raped over 20 women. When I was deep in my cycle, I would drive the streets looking for a victim. Now that I've been released after five years in prison, I'm participating in a community treatment program for sex offenders.

My therapist taught me how to use thought-stopping. I have been trained to say "STOP!" and to refute my inappropriate thoughts rationally whenever thoughts or fantasies about rape or victims come into my mind.

First, I kept a thought log to become more aware about my thinking. Then I identified my unhealthy thoughts: getting a woman alone and raping her. I discovered that I spent a *lot* of time and energy thinking about rape and feeding my fantasies. I would catch myself several times a day thinking rape thoughts about women I knew, about driving and looking for women, or getting women alone and forcing them to have sex. One night I broke my therapy contract and had a beer. Then I found that when I was drinking alcohol—even one beer—I had many more deviant thoughts than usual.

That one beer was enough to scare me. I was able to catch myself as inappropriate thoughts came into my mind. I began to stop those thoughts as soon as I detected them by telling myself "STOP!" and countering the deviant thoughts. I thought about the consequences if I committed another offense: what it was like to be in prison, the harm I caused my victims, the shame and embarrassment I caused my wife and my victims' families, and the legal consequences of reoffending. It worked then, and it just keeps working to help me keep myself safe.

Figure 1

1. Awareness

2. Catch Thoughts

3. Stop Thoughts

4. Counter Thoughts

Chapter 6 Assignments

∽ Do not write in this workbook ∽

29. Watch your speech and thoughts for several days. Write down your most common verbal or mental expressions. Note both the positive and the negative expressions, both are very important. Examples: "Oh shit"; "Who gives a damn"; "So what"; "I don't know"; etc.

30. Try sitting quietly in a room for 15 minutes. Focus on your thoughts and count them. Try to count each idea or image that enters your mind. Write down how many thoughts you counted. See if you can sort your thoughts into categories, for example, physical sensations (hungry, tired, leg aches), emotions (bored, angry, happy, numb), fantasies or wishes (I'd like to ...). Which thoughts come in words? Which thoughts come in pictures? Report your discoveries.

31. Identify several undesirable thought patterns you would like to work on.

32. Practice thought-stopping with the thoughts you identified above. You will have several insights about the process; write them down and share them.

33. Describe the positive thoughts you will use to replace your negative thoughts.

Review your answers to these assignments with your therapist and your group. If you are working on your own, share your answers with a friend or person you trust.

7.

Positive Self-Talk

HOW YOU TALK TO YOURSELF IN YOUR MIND affects your behavior, your attitudes, and your self-image. What you say to yourself in your mind is called *self-talk*. Self-talk is very powerful. Suspicious, angry self-talk can make you a suspicious, angry person—someone no one wants to be near. Enthusiastic, encouraging self-talk can keep you going when everyone else has given up. Positive self-talk can help make you successful and liked.

Without even realizing it, you talk to yourself in positive or negative ways every day of your life. Your self-talk determines how you feel and how the world looks to you. It is like looking at a picture of the sun on the horizon. People with positive self-talk feel the sun is rising and a new day is about to begin with lots of possibilities. People with negative self-talk feel the day is almost over and a time of darkness and despair is beginning. When they look at a half-filled glass of water, their negative self-talk convinces them to see it as half empty.

Negative Self-Talk

There are two basic types of negative self-talk: the kind that justifies unhealthy behavior, and the kind that makes you feel worthless or insignificant.

Negative self-talk that justifies unhealthy behavior may sound like the following:

- I deserve to be able to look at pornography.
- Smoking marijuana really isn't abusing drugs.
- One drink won't do any damage.
- I can go to the park if I don't talk to kids.
- Driving alone at night won't affect me.

- I can drive my car if I want to. It's my car.
- I brought my kids into the world. I can spank them all I want.

This type of negative self-talk makes you feel angry and resentful. It starts off with false assumptions about what you deserve, what is owed to you, or why it is okay to do what you want to do even when it is wrong. You can resist this kind of thinking the first few times it happens, but after hours or days of it you will give in. Negative self-talk like this quickly gets you into trouble.

Negative self-talk that makes you feel worthless or insignificant is a sign that you may be experiencing AVE (Abstinence Violation Effect), and may sound like these statements:

- Why bother trying, nothing goes right for me anyhow.
- It doesn't pay to be honest. I'll always be the loser.
- No one else cares, so why should I?
- Everything I try ends in failure.
- I'm sure stupid.
- No one would want to talk to me.
- I'm a worthless SOB.

A full day of negative self-talk will make you feel you deserve the worst. It will make you think any positive effort on your part is worthless. You begin to ask, "Why not give up?" Most negative self-talk is distorted and based on irrational thoughts and beliefs.

Positive Self-Talk

Reality-based positive self-talk consists of *rational* thoughts and beliefs. It reinforces what you know is

31

right and helps keep you thinking clearly. Positive self-talk encourages you and makes you feel capable of achieving your goals.

Positive self-talk can stop destructive behaviors and start healthy ones. By itself, positive self-talk will reward and encourage you, and best of all, it enhances the effectiveness of other intervention techniques. When what you say to yourself is positive and inspiring, it helps you work toward accomplishing your goals and dreams. When your dream is to recover from the destruction of your life caused by your sexual deviancy, you will recover if you work hard and give yourself realistic credit for your work. You will not keep yourself safe and offense-free if you consistently talk to yourself in a discouraging and despairing way.

Two Types of Positive Self-Talk

There are two kinds of positive self-talk: talk that enhances your self-esteem, and talk that encourages healthy behavior.

Positive self-talk that enhances self-esteem may sound like these statements:

- I can do it.
- I did a good job.
- It was hard but I stuck to it.
- I followed through, great!
- I'm really pleased with myself.
- I'm delighted I passed the class.
- It was great getting praised.
- I deserved the reward I got.
- I was a good person today.
- I really am intelligent enough.
- I am glad I could help him.

When you are filled with this type of talk, you feel good about yourself and what you have done. When you feel good about who you are, it is possible to do more, be more tolerant, and be generous. The more confident, tolerant, and generous you are in spirit and energy, the more people listen to and respect you.

The second type of positive self-talk encourages healthy behavior. It may sound like:

- A lot of people have urges. I don't have to give in to mine; as I work on changing them, they will pass with time.
- I am going to make mistakes from time to time. I can learn from my mistakes and improve my abilities.
- I have many qualities that my friends like, such as patience, understanding, and forgiveness.
- I made the right decision by turning down the beer and the joint.
- I can learn these interventions and improve myself.
- I can control my temper.
- I won't let them get to me.

This kind of self-talk helps keep you going. When you are thinking positively, you are not thrown off by frustrating events. You will be able to resist temptation and learn from your mistakes.

Positive self-talk is an essential part of most interventions. Without it you will not follow through with your plans or dreams. Everyone has positive qualities, strengths, and abilities, including you. But you may not be skilled at giving yourself credit for positive qualities. As you practice, you will become more skilled. Start right now by giving yourself credit for reading this chapter. Good job!

Changing Negative to Positive Self-Talk

Honesty, as mentioned earlier, is essential to recovery. You cannot shift from negative self-talk to positive self-talk if you have not been honest about your past and who you are. When you know your life is based on lies, deceit, and false fronts, your positive self-talk becomes another lie.

Awareness is another essential factor in changing from negative to positive self-talk. What is your current self-talk like? What do you say to yourself about difficult situations, responsibilities, opportunities, and limitations? Once you figure out what your negative self-talk is, you will be ready to make a change to positive self-talk.

To figure out what your negative self-talk is, consider what you say to yourself when you are: frustrated, tired, denied what you want, disappointed, faced with a hard job to do, or facing something you don't want to do. At these times you probably say something negative about yourself, your task, or someone else. Listen to your thoughts for the next week and see what you tell yourself.

Plan positive things to say. Plan what you are going to say and when you are going to say it. For example, you might plan to give yourself credit for being patient. Plan what you will tell yourself about patience: "I did it! I kept my patience." "When I'm patient, I'm strong." Patient Patrick had to work hard to get this one, but the reward was worth it:

My name is Patrick. One weekend I agreed to help some friends move. I showed up on time, even though it was 6 am on a Saturday and I'd been out late at a meeting the night before. No one else showed up. I waited, and waited, and waited some more. Was I mad! I just kept thinking to myself, "I was a jerk to believe them. I'm really pissed off. I'm a fool. Those idiots, I'll never help them again." At 6:30 I went home. I was angry with myself and with my "so-called" friends. I guess I spent most of the day angry and upset, picturing those guys laughing at me and enjoying what a joke they had played on me. I was giving myself a hard time for being so stupid. Later that day I got a phone call from one of my friends: they had car trouble and were at the mechanic's waiting for a part.

I don't know, I guess I just lost it: I let my negative thinking and anger take over and lost a whole day that I could have enjoyed doing something else. My friends weren't late on purpose to humiliate me. I understood for the first time that my anger was not based on facts, but on my own negative self-talk. But I remembered something I had learned in my therapy: I could change my feelings by changing my thinking. I decided I would try it on my negative thinking. Each time I felt frustrated, I would interrupt my intolerant thinking by telling myself, "I can be patient for five more minutes."

The next Monday at work, I was expecting Luke, my supervisor, to talk to me about some job specifications. I waited. By 10 am Luke had not spoken to me. I started to get upset, thinking, "He's not going to talk to me. I was dumb for asking. I never get recognized around here." Each time I noticed that my fists were clenched, my jaw hurt, and my face felt hot, I realized I was getting angry. So I told myself, "I can be patient for five more minutes" over and over for most of the day. I managed to stay calm and optimistic minute by minute.

At 5 o'clock I had given up on getting the specs in time to start the job, but I still wasn't angry. I felt like I had won a victory over my negative thinking. I had controlled my anger and impatience. I knew I didn't have to feel humiliated or victimized by other people not following *my* schedule. My co-workers couldn't get an automatic angry reaction out of me by being late.

When Luke finally came over, I was still calm. He told me, "I'm sorry I couldn't talk with you earlier—it was a pretty bad day. But every time I wanted to blow my top because the schedule was being held up, I'd look at you just going about your business. I figured that if you, with your temper, could handle me being late, I could handle adjusting the schedule. Thanks. Let's meet first thing in the morning." I was really surprised!

You can make your world a better place by how you think about it. Positive self-talk improves how you see the world and how the world sees you.

Chapter 7 Assignments

34. Consider your typical negative thinking that allows you to *behave* in ways you are not happy with. If you think carefully, you will find many examples of negative self-talk—write down at least 10.

35. Write down your typical negative self-talk that makes you *feel* less worthwhile. This type of self-talk is like self-criticism. Listen to the inner critical voice telling you about all the ways you fail. Come up with 20 examples.

36. Write down 10 ways you can tell yourself what is right with you, so you can feel better and achieve more.

37. Write down the opposite, positive side of the negative thoughts you described in Assignments #34 and #35. For example, if your negative self-talk was, "I always fail at everything," write down something you did not fail at.

Review your answers to these assignments with your therapist and your group. If you are working on your own, share your answers with a friend or person you trust.

8.

Relaxation

RELAXATION IS A VALUABLE INTERVENTION for everyone. Relaxation exercises allow you to get a fresh view of your day and your life. You may get so involved in what you are doing, thinking, or feeling that you can't see what else is going on. Doing something to relax often will help you reflect on your life and show you better ways to be in the future.

You probably felt stressed and tense before you acted out. The stress may have come from pressure at work, anger in your relationship, problems with money, or just everyday life. When your internal tension increases, you become more irritable, less patient, and more critical. Learning to recognize and reduce your stress is often a way to stop your problems from getting worse.

Recognizing Stress

The first sign of stress is tension in your body. Tight muscles in your forehead, jaw, shoulders, back, neck, and stomach are signs you are tense. Other signs may be a faster heartbeat, rapid or shallow breathing, headaches, and fatigue. You get tired faster when you are tense because tension uses up energy. When you are under stress for a long time, your body tension may make you feel exhausted even though you haven't been doing anything strenuous.

When you are stressed, and either don't know it or don't know what to do about it, you may fall into old, unhealthy habits. Automatic Al has an old habit of using food inappropriately.

When Al's stress increases he automatically heads for food. You may have a similar pattern with food, alcohol, anger, depression, wild behavior, gambling, or sex.

My name is Al, and I learned as a child that eating is a great way to relax. Food feels good and tastes good going down, and when I'm stressed out, eating always makes me feel better. When I was a kid, it was clear that no one expected me to do anything hard or upsetting while I was eating. As an adult, I still think of eating to help me deal with stress. For example, when I'm paying bills I get a quart of Ben & Jerry's ice cream to get me through. When I get hassled at work, I usually go out for a special meal to cheer me up and calm me down. I know I need help to change these patterns, so that's why I joined an overeaters support group.

Suppose you have a pattern like Al's, but instead of using food you use sex. When you are tense you start thinking of sex as a way to relax. You begin using masturbation, pornography, or prostitutes as ways to relax. Choosing a sexual way to deal with nonsexual feelings is inappropriate because it feeds your problem with deviant sexual behavior and such choices contribute to your deviant cycle.

As you learned when you studied your deviant cycle, trying to escape from stress (or other problems) in unhealthy ways leads to more problems. You move faster and deeper into your cycle as these additional problems increase your worry, anxiety, confusion, frustration, fear, and anger. You are under more and more stress. As your stress increases, your thinking becomes less clear. You feel in pain and out of control. You are more likely to act out your deviant behavior as you try to escape from your painful feelings.

Healthy relaxation can help you *control* your tension but will not *cure* it. By using relaxation techniques, you can think more clearly about solutions to your problems instead of sinking under a snowballing burden of stress and tension.

Relaxation Techniques

There are many ways to relax. For some people, an active sport gives them a sense of relaxation. For others, watching TV or a movie may be a way of handling stress. For still others, a long talk with a good friend is comforting and stress-reducing. However there are several techniques you can learn that may be more efficient and healthier than what you currently use. Try out the one described in detail below.

Progressive Deep Relaxation

1. Choose a quiet place or time. It is best if you can be undisturbed for about a half-hour.
2. To relax completely, lie down where you can be fully stretched out and supported. However, if lying down is inappropriate or if you fall asleep when you lie down, sit in a comfortable chair.
3. Start by looking at a point in front of you and allow your eyes to relax. It does not matter if they are open or closed, but most people close them.
4. Take in a long, slow, deep breath and let it out slowly.
5. Tell yourself, "I'm going to relax for a half-hour. I will let myself do this. I do not need to do anything else for the next few minutes."
6. Tense your toes for 10 to 20 seconds while breathing in; then relax your toes completely while breathing out. Notice the difference between the feeling of tension and the feeling of relaxation. Each time you breathe out, say to yourself, "I'm becoming more relaxed."

Next, tense your feet for 10 to 20 seconds while breathing in, then relax them while breathing out. Each time you breathe out, let go of all tension and tell yourself, "I'm more relaxed."

Continue this process of tensing and breathing in, then relaxing and breathing out for each part of your body from your feet up: legs, thighs, pelvis, abdomen, back, hands, forearms, upper arms, shoulders, neck, face, and head. After completing this process, mentally scan over your entire body and see if you can find any areas that are still tense. If so, repeat the deep breathing with tensing and relaxing of that area a few more times.

7. After going through your body, sit quietly and repeat a single word or phrase repeatedly, like, "relax," or "peace." If you have a spiritual practice you might say a one-line prayer over and over. When you notice your mind wandering just bring it back to your chosen word or phrase. Distracting thoughts or worries will try to run through your mind. Concentrating on a single relaxing thought or phrase will help you not to start worrying.

Relaxation can be a useful addition to other treatment techniques. Escape coupled with relaxation is easier and more effective. Visual imagery, which you will learn about in the next chapter, is impossible without relaxation. Relapse rehearsal, thought-stopping, and positive self-talk are all enhanced by relaxation.

Chapter 8 Assignments

∽ **Do not write in this workbook** ∾

38. Write down how your body lets you know you are tense. Describe the sensations from your head to your feet.

39. Write about the ways you have used to reduce your tension. Discuss both your healthy and unhealthy ways.

40. Practice the Progressive Deep Relaxation technique once a day every day. Everyone finds ways that work best for them. *EACH DAY* write about your experience.

Review your answers to these assignments with your therapist and your group. If you are working on your own, share your answers with a friend or person you trust.

9.

Imagery as a Coping Strategy & Intervention

VISUAL IMAGERY MEANS SEEING PICTURES in your mind. It is what you do when you imagine something. It is easy to do. Right now, close your eyes and imagine a dog. What color is the dog? Is it long- or short-haired? The picture of the dog in your mind is a visual image. The pictures you see may be quick, as when a scene flashes up from your past. Or they may come to you slowly and last a long time, as in a daydream or fantasy. Visual imagery, like thought, affects you powerfully. A visual image of a lifelong project could change the direction of your whole life. For example, a visual image of the house you want to build could influence you for years, until you finally build your dream house. A visual image of a deviant sexual behavior could destroy your life.

Deviant Fantasy Is Visual Imagery

Deviant sexual fantasies are a type of visual imagery that can be dangerous. When you masturbate to your deviant fantasies, you make them stronger. Before your sexual crimes you probably engaged in fantasy rehearsal, using visual imagery and deviant self-talk, and often strengthened by masturbation.

The more you allow yourself to think about a deviant fantasy, the more real it seems. For example, you may have a visual image in your mind of the woman next door. Suppose you mentally undress her and imagine having sex with her. After playing with this fantasy for a while you may begin to believe she really is sexually attracted to you. After all, in your mind you have often rehearsed how you want her to respond. Because of your fantasies, one day you approach her in an overly familiar way, like she was an old lover instead of a stranger. She could take one

look at you, and think, "What a slimeball," and avoid you afterward. You may not understand why she has begun to avoid you, since you had earlier fantasized a sexual relationship. If you fail to see that you have already begun acting improperly on your fantasy, you may use her "rejection" to fuel your anger. When you mix that kind of fantasy with anger and drugs or alcohol, you are setting yourself up to rape.

Visual Imagery Is Automatic

Visual imagery for many people is automatic. Read the following description:

> You are on a tropical beach dotted with palm trees. There are a few people walking on the beach. Looking out over the ocean you see a sailboat. What color is its sail? What color is the water?

Most people have ready answers like, the sail is white. The water is blue. But how would you know that? Probably as you were reading that description you had a mental picture of the beach in your mind. When you were asked the questions, perhaps you "saw" the colors in your mind. If you did not already do so, take a moment and close your eyes. Imagine a beach scene and ask yourself what color the sand and the sail are. Hear the sound of the waves collapsing to wash over the sand and the gulls calling. Smell the warm, salty air. Feel the sun pour over your back.

Visual imagery is easy to produce. In fact it is so easy and common that we tend to dismiss it: "He's wasting time with daydreams." "He's off in another world." It is true sometimes people get caught up in dreams and are unable to face reality. But usually the problem is that they have not learned to use visual imagery effectively. Visual imagery is very powerful, especially when other senses (taste, touch, hearing, and smell) are also involved.

Using Visual Imagery

Visual imagery can be used in several ways. It can help you practice how to get out of difficult situations, rehearse new behaviors, or change an arousing deviant scene into an aversive one. Visual imagery can help you relax, or show you an inner dream for your future. It is a wonderful tool.

Relaxation with Visual Imagery

Relaxation helps you use visual imagery effectively. In the last chapter you learned how to relax your body using Progressive Deep Relaxation. You can also learn to relax using visual imagery. For most people, a combination of both visual imagery and Progressive Deep Relaxation works best.

The following is a simple form of visual imagery for relaxation. Read the entire exercise before practicing it. You may want to read it several times to help you memorize the basic process. Another good way to use this exercise is to tape record yourself reading it in a slow, soothing voice. Then play the tape back when you want help to relax.

1. As with the Progressive Deep Relaxation exercise, find a quiet place and time. You may sit or lie down, depending on your needs.

2. Begin by closing your eyes and taking several slow deep breaths. Slow your breathing down to four or five deep breaths per minute. Practice deep breathing for three to five minutes. Keep your thoughts on relaxation. Imagine that each time you breathe out, you are releasing tension and becoming more relaxed.

3. Close your eyes and imagine that behind your forehead is a blank empty screen. On this screen look down at yourself as if you were watching yourself from the ceiling. Imagine seeing yourself relax.

4. Continue breathing deeply, and with every breath imagine breathing tension out of your body. Try to see the tension as it leaves. It may look like a dark or colored cloud. Each time you breathe out, see a dark cloud of tension being blown out of your body.

5. Now see your feet on your mental screen. Imagine each muscle becoming relaxed with no stress or strain. See the dark cloud of tension as it gently leaves your feet, travels up your legs, through your body, and into your lungs. Each time you breathe out, you can see the cloud of tension leaving your body along with your breath. As you look down upon your feet on the screen, you see them become more and more relaxed.

6. Now imagine your legs becoming more relaxed. On your mental screen you see the muscles of your calves and thighs becoming more relaxed, as you watch the dark cloud of tension traveling into your chest, and leaving with each breath. As you look down upon your body you see your legs and feet being completely relaxed.

7. Look at your abdomen now. Relax your stomach, hips, and genitals with each breath. See the tension move from the lower part of your body into your lungs. See the darkness leaving with each breath.

8. Do the same with your fingers, hands, arms, neck, shoulders, and head. Continue to focus on seeing the tension leave and allowing relaxation to replace it. Finally, relax the muscles in your chest and lungs. Watch your tight muscles loosening up and all the dark tension completely leaving your lungs with each breath.

9. Now imagine there is a golden light of health entering your body. With each breath let this light fill more and more of your body until every space is full and light.

You now know one way to relax using visual imagery. There are many others. Visual imagery can be used as a type of controlled daydream, where you can see yourself in a very relaxed and comfortable place. Suppose the earlier example of the beach scene were expanded: you could gradually relax into the pleasant, nonthreatening images. Seeing a pleasant, untroubled scene can help you calm down.

Aversive Visual Imagery (Covert Sensitization)

What if the scene you see in your mind is not pleasant, as in a nightmare? When you have a nightmare, you feel tense and scared, and you want to get away. A nightmare is a form of *aversive visual imagery*. While *aversive visual imagery* is rarely used, it can be very helpful when it is used consciously in a technique like *Covert Sensitization*. "Covert" means hidden; mentally imagining something is hidden. "Sensitization" means making you more aware of something.

You use *aversive visual imagery* for *Covert Sensitization* when you want to create a feeling of wanting to get away (aversion). For example, suppose you have fantasies of sex with little girls, fantasies that you know are clearly wrong. When you notice one of these fantasies starting, you intervene with a mental picture of something very negative—like doing time in the state penitentiary. The fear of doing time may be enough to help you chase the fantasy out of your mind. When the visual imagery is strong, detailed, realistic, and carries lots of emotion, it can help you stop thinking about deviant sex as exciting and start thinking about the unpleasant or aversive consequences. **NOTE: Since using Covert Sensitization incorrectly may lead to problems, we recommend that you not use this technique without consulting an experienced therapist.**

Rehearsing with Visual Imagery

Visual imagery can be used to rehearse a behavior, such as responding to an interviewer's questions with confidence and self-assurance, or a new skill, for example, escaping from a risk situation. Using visual imagery for rehearsal has several steps:

1. Relaxation: use any of the relaxation techniques you've learned.
2. Clear your mind of extra thoughts. Imagining the empty screen is one way to do this.
3. Get a clear picture in your mind of the scene you want to rehearse.
4. Imagine yourself in the scene performing each step of your task well.
5. If you notice any anxiety or tension developing while you see the scene, go back to the beginning, relax again, then start over.
6. Keep repeating this process until you are able to see yourself successfully run through the entire scene without fear or tension.

Relaxed Roger used visual imagery to rehearse his upcoming job interview with Big Blue Machine Tools:

My name is Roger, and I've been learning to use Progressive Deep Relaxation and visual imagery. Two days before my interview, I got myself relaxed, then cleared my mind and set up my mental screen. I pictured Big Blue's front office building, where I'd have my job interview. I saw myself in my best navy blue suit with my maroon tie. The sun flashed off my spit-shined shoes as I saw myself walking up to the building and stepping inside. I watched on my mental screen as I strode confidently into the receptionist's area. I imagined the self-assurance in my voice as I told the receptionist, "I have an appointment with Ms. Shay." Now don't get me wrong—I didn't turn overnight into Tom Selleck or Robert DeNiro. That was really me on my mental screen: bald spot and glasses and everything. I kept picturing me at my best, but I was still me, Roger.

While I was picturing myself waiting, I noticed I was feeling tense and scared. I stopped the scene and started over with my relaxation exercise before once again picturing myself outside the door of Big Blue.

Finally, I was able to picture myself waiting in the reception area without being tense. Then I pictured the door opening, and I walked calmly and confidently into the office and sat down. I imagined the kinds of questions Ms. Shay would ask: about my background, education, experience, goals, and my reasons for applying to Big Blue. I figured she might ask what I could do for the company if she hired me. I visualized myself giving good, well-thought-out answers. I saw us shake hands and walk out, knowing that I had done a good interview.

Imagery will be used in several interventions in following chapters.

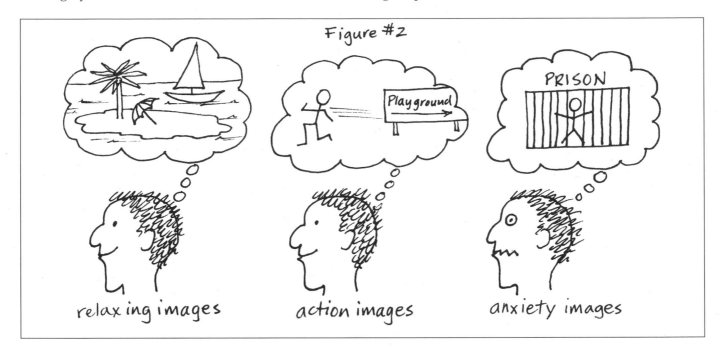

Figure #2

relaxing images   action images   anxiety images

Chapter 9 Assignments

⌘ Do not write in this workbook ⌘

41. Practice using visual imagery with relaxation every day for a week. *EACH DAY* write about what you discover while using this process.

42. Write down some unpleasant scenes you could use to intervene in your deviant thoughts. Describe the scene in detail, the location, what happens, who is present, and how you felt. The details should be realistic enough to let you feel the same emotions as if it were really happening.

43. Write in detail about a scene that shows a new behavior that would replace your deviancy and that you would like to add to your life. Give details about how you would look and act and how you wish others to respond to you.

44. Use the scene from Assignment #43 to rehearse the new behavior at least once a day for a week. Describe what you learned from this exercise. Did it change your behavior in your current situation? If so, how?

Review your answers to these assignments with your therapist and your group. If you are working on your own, share your answers with a friend or person you trust.

10.

Enhancing Empathy

TREATMENT IS ABOUT NEVER AGAIN having victims or being in trouble with the legal system. One way to achieve these goals is to learn to feel what it feels like to be a victim. Learning to feel what others feel is called *empathy*.

Have you ever identified with a character in a movie? If you did, it was probably because the character was expressing something that touched your emotions. Maybe you felt the "same pain" as the character. You felt as if you knew what it was like to be the character. Understanding how someone else feels is called *empathy*. People who are in pain, yet go out of their way to help others, probably do so out of empathy. They know how the other person feels and want to help.

Empathy is the ability to put yourself into someone else's shoes, to see the world through their eyes, and experience what they are experiencing. Learning to feel empathy doesn't "happen" overnight: you have to develop it by practicing over and over, just as you have to do pushups over and over to develop your muscles. You can learn empathy by feeling deeply and paying close attention to the feelings of others. You need to be sharp and aware.

Take a moment to think about something that happened to you in the past that was hurtful, unpleasant, or saddening. If you wanted others to help you and understand your feelings, what you wanted from them was empathy.

When you care about someone you are more likely to feel empathy for them. When you empathize with your wife or womanfriend, you understand how she feels. If you really knew and cared about what victims felt before, during, and after your crimes, you would not have committed them. Consider Chilly Willy's case:

Y'all can call me Willy. I'm a rapist, been caught, convicted, and sent to prison, where they strongly suggested I join this sex-offender treatment group. So I did—thought it would look good on my jacket, and besides, I'm so bored in here, I'll try anything once. Last week, we had to watch this film about rape victims, then talk about it in group. The therapy guy asks me what those women in the film felt, and I just tell him straight out, "How should I know? I ain't a woman." Then the leader tries to tell me that it was real plain because the women *said* on the screen they felt pain, and ashamed, and angry, and like they were humiliated. Then, he asks me if I thought it was true what they were saying on the film about their feelings. I already been kinda mouthy, so I just hang my head over, shrug my shoulders, and kinda mumble, "Yeah, I guess so." This leader just wouldn't let up on me. He asks me if I can *describe* how the women's pain felt. I'm real quiet and polite this time—if he don't get it the first time I tell him that I'm no woman, I ain't gonna tell him a second time. So I just say, "No. I mean, I don't *know* these ladies, and I don't even *like* 'em, so why should I give a hang *what* they feel?" Then the leader says to me, "If you don't care about how these women feel, what's going to keep you from raping another woman you don't know or like, especially if you think you could get away with it without getting caught?" There wasn't anything else for me to say but, "I don't know. Nothing, I guess!"

Some offenders enjoy inflicting pain on other people because it makes them feel powerful: the offender can make some one else feel feelings he doesn't want. Other offenders (for example, rapists who believe the myth that women enjoy rape and pedophiles who say they really "love" children) choose not to recognize or accept that their behavior causes emotional, spiritual, and/or physical pain in their victims: if they understood how much pain they caused to people they say they *care* about, they would stop. Caring and empathy go together. You feel affection, warmth, sympathy, and kindness when you really care for someone, and you can imagine how things feel to them. You can feel *empathic* with them. True empathy is feeling care and concern for people whether you know them or not. It is a concern for life and a respect for others and their lives. Empathy does not exclude strangers.

Developing Empathy

Most men who have no empathy have shut off their own feelings of fear, shame, pain, confidence, and joy. When you shut off painful feelings, you also lose the ability to experience positive feelings. Consider Stonewall Sam's case:

> Yeah, okay, I'll tell you the story, but I'm going to do it *my* way. Once upon a time there was a young boy named **Sam**. He got into trouble in a class one day the year he was 12 and had to sit in detention. He was mad, so he mouthed off to the detention monitor. The monitor grabbed him and took him into the boiler room, made him strip, and raped him. Sam was only a kid, so he was real scared he was going to die. Then he was ashamed because that man had done this awful thing to him and he could never tell anyone about it. He felt out of control, powerless, weak, and defenseless. He hated these feelings and the rapist who caused them. He hated his parents for not doing more to help. He hated the school where it happened.
>
> After being raped, that boy Sam never wanted to feel such terrible feelings again. He figured out that the only one who *didn't* feel horrible was the rapist, who acted strong, powerful, and in control. This kid Sam decided that from now on, *he* was going to be like the rapist. He hated the weak, powerless, and vulnerable parts of himself. After years of hating these feelings, our boy Sam learned never to feel vulnerable or in pain. He totally blocked out any sense of empathy. By the time he was leaving high school, this young man Sam could rape someone, leave, and just forget it. He just didn't care. **My name is Sam.**

For Sam to develop empathy he must learn to feel *and accept* his own powerlessness. Accepting it means being willing to know it exists and to feel it. When Sam accepts his feelings of fear, powerlessness, and inadequacy, he will be able to feel the pain of others. When he accepts his painful feelings, he will more fully experience joy and happiness, too. You can only empathize with feelings you are willing to experience yourself. If you are unwilling to feel shame, you can't empathize with someone else's shame.

Think back to your sexual offense and what you did to your victim. Maybe you felt remorse, guilt, or shame after you committed your crime. If so, those feelings could be the start of empathy. Another way to start learning empathy is to imagine a time when you felt terrible. It may have been when you were beaten up, arrested, or went bankrupt. Perhaps you were sexually or physically victimized yourself when you were young. Whatever it was, allow yourself to remember the intensity of those feelings. Still another way is to imagine you are a victim of a crime. Think about the old feelings you had and allow them to become stronger. Victims feel intensely. No matter how intensely painful, or sorrowful, or depressed you are about your crimes as an offender, your victims felt and feel worse.

The focus of empathy is not how *you* feel, it is how *others* feel. The only way you can understand the depth of their feelings is to feel deeply yourself and *then put yourself in the other person's place.* Think of how you would feel if you were experiencing what they are experiencing.

Feeling empathy is not about giving up power and control in your life. It takes a strong person to care about others, to feel what they feel, and to be aware enough to want to help. It does *not* mean indulging in pity.

Feeling sad for someone else's misfortune is a form of empathy; feeling sorry for yourself is self-pity. Self-pity keeps you from looking at the effects of your crimes. It enables you to continue your deviant behavior. Self-pity does not help you change; it encourages you to blame others for your misfortune. When you're wrapped up in self-pity, you focus on what you don't like and how everyone else is better off. You use it to feed your anger and greed instead of making productive changes.

Note: Disgust about your crime is an appropriate and realistic feeling for an offender. Being disgusted with the pain you have caused and the people you have affected is a step in the right direction. But, it works only when you can use this feeling to motivate yourself to change. Without a commitment to change, being disgusted with yourself is another form of self-pity, and it only feeds your deviant cycle.

One way to demonstrate your empathy and care is to contribute to a local agency that helps victims (mental health, rape crisis, or battered women's groups, for example). Giving money to help victims get counseling or donating time to a community service project—without expecting a pat on the back for it—shows that you care about your victim's future.

Empathy Is Thinking Before You Act

At times you will be overwhelmed with angry, upset, or discouraged feelings. When you're "in a bad mood," it's easy to lash out at whoever is handy, dumping your feelings on them regardless of who they are or what they've done. Before you lash out, stop. Take a moment to think about the other person before you act. When you faced someone in a bad mood, how did you feel when they dumped on you? How do you *wish* they had talked to you? Learning to think of the other person before dumping your feelings is one way to develop empathy.

Suppose a co-worker is angry with you and feels his anger is justified. Try to put yourself in his place and think about the situation from his perspective. Imagine for a moment that you completely understand and agree with his anger. How do you think your behavior looks through his eyes? If you were your co-worker, how would you want to be treated? How do you want others to talk to you? Think about

how you would like to receive feedback. Practice getting feedback with the next person you meet.

Share With Others

When you are feeling lonely and depressed, sad or discouraged, down and frustrated, take the time to talk with others. The more you share your emotions and thoughts with good people (who can be found everywhere, even in a maximum security prison), the more they will share with you. Of course, it is important to think carefully and honestly about how to choose supportive companions with whom you can share. Sharing leads to understanding and develops empathy.

When you share your feelings and thoughts with an empathetic person, you learn how others respond. Think about what your most supportive friends do to help you feel understood. What do they say? How do they reassure you? What do they do to show they care about you? See what is helpful for you, then use this experience to help others. **NOTE:** Empathy is not the same as *enabling*. An enabler—or a "sliding partner"—may support everything you do, even when it is unhealthy or criminal. People with empathy understand your feelings and at the same time give you honest feedback that holds you accountable for your actions.

You cannot develop empathy when you withdraw from people; you must be involved with people. Living in a vacuum leaves you empty, despairing, and suspicious. Isolation can kill empathy.

As you reach out and begin to connect with your community, you will develop friendships and meaningful relationships, and people will begin to feel more comfortable and trusting of you. When this starts to happen (remember, it takes time), people may come to you for help of one kind or another. They may just need someone to listen to them talk. They may want more substantial help. Take the time to learn to help and be a source of comfort for someone. Practice care and concern for others.

Chapter 10 Assignment

⌒ **Do not write in this workbook** ⌒

45. Part of treatment is to learn to feel empathy with victims. Focus on understanding the effects of your crime on your victims. Try to put yourself in your victims' place. Write out your answers to the following questions:

    1. What *physical feelings* do you think your victims felt just before, during, and after your sexual crimes?
    2. What do you think they *thought* just before, during, and after your crimes?
    3. What *emotions* do you think they felt just before, during, and after your crimes?
    4. What do you think your victims are now experiencing physically, emotionally, and mentally?
    5. How do you think your crimes affected their families?
    6. Think about someone you dislike. Imagine how they feel physically, mentally, and emotionally.
    7. Think about either the child protection or social worker who helped your victim, or the policeman who was involved with your case. How do you think they felt physically, mentally, and emotionally when they interviewed you and your victims?

NOTE: Because empathy is not one of your personality strengths (or you would not have committed your crime), spend some extra time with this assignment. But remember that the quality of empathy in what you write matters the most, whether you write 3 pages or 30.

Review your answers to this assignment with your therapist and your group. If you are working on your own, share your answers with a friend or person you trust.

11.
Relapse Rehearsal

NOW THAT YOU HAVE LEARNED and practiced several interventions, you are ready to integrate them with *Relapse Rehearsal*. Relapse Rehearsal is like a fire drill: it teaches you what to do in case of emergency, in this case, a lapse. Everyone has *lapses*, times when he slips back into a habitual emotion, thought pattern, fantasy, or behavior that contributed to his offense. *Relapse Rehearsal* is about how to cope with lapses and risk situations. There are several ways of doing Relapse Rehearsal. Perhaps the best way is to rehearse appropriate thinking and behavior in group therapy; the therapist and group members can give you feedback about whether your plans will work. But many of you reading this workbook don't have access to a treatment group; therefore the Relapse Rehearsal technique discussed here is one you can practice either in a group or on your own. In this technique, you use visual imagery mentally to practice successful responses to lapses and high-risk situations. By rehearsing in your mind coping with your lapses and with the AVE, you can exercise the intervention skills you have learned.

Why Rehearse Coping with a Lapse?

Rehearsing coping with a lapse or a high-risk situation may sound silly, but to use interventions well you must practice or rehearse them. The focus is on using a *successful coping strategy* for dealing with a lapse. Solving a problem during your mental rehearsal gives you a feeling of success and prepares you to succeed in the future. The more you practice *solving* risk situations, the better prepared you will be to succeed. Knowing ahead of time that you will lapse and that you have rehearsed the skills to cope with it successfully, helps you to respond effectively. Coping successfully with

lapses prevents you from using the Abstinence Violation Effect (feeling like a failure, giving up, and going on a binge) to move deeper into your deviant cycle.

Relapse Rehearsal: The Method

You can learn Relapse Rehearsal without the guidance of a therapist, but professional advice and supervision are *highly* recommended. Relapse Rehearsal is designed to help you avoid or escape a risk situation *before* you experience a relapse. There are five steps in this technique: (1) identify and write down your risk situations; (2) choose an intervention you will use for the risk situation; (3) relax and see the visual image of yourself in the risk situation; (4) in your mind visualize yourself using the intervention to solve the problem posed by the risk situation; and (5) give yourself encouragement with positive self-talk.

Identify Risk Situations.

To identify your risk situations, write down any thought, feeling, behavior, or environment that contributes to your deviant cycle. Review your answers to Assignment #23 in Chapter Four if you need help. Examples might include picking up hitch-hikers, using pornography, being alone with a child, abusing alcohol, being depressed, avoiding people, or being angry.

Choose an Intervention.

Think about one of your risk situations. Now decide which intervention would be the most effective way to handle it. Think about the intervention in detail. For example, if you decide to use *thought-stopping*, think of exactly what you would say and do. If you decide to use *escape*, again think of what you would say and do. Get all the details firmly in your mind.

Visualize Yourself in the Risk Situation

Go to a comfortable place where you won't be disturbed, as if you were going to do a relaxation session. Once you are relaxed, visualize yourself in the risk situation. Imagine the details. For example, suppose you are an exhibitionist and your risk situation was driving down a wooded road used by joggers. See the color of the trees and how wide the shoulder of the road is. Notice the jogging path, is it straight or curved? Notice the young woman jogger, ask yourself what color her hair and clothes are. Lastly, see yourself driving along and looking at the woman.

NOTE: Do *not* let yourself imagine arousing scenes. Stop the scene and use your intervention *before* you become aroused enough to imagine acting out.

Mentally Rehearse Using the Intervention

Picture yourself using the intervention. In this example, suppose you want to use *escape* and *thought-stopping*. In your mind, see yourself driving down the road, recognizing the risk situation, and deciding to escape from it. In your rehearsal you immediately turn around. Then imagine using thought-stopping (to avoid thinking about exposing). You might say to yourself, "STOP! I told my wife I would be home soon. I'll call her and let her know where I am and when to expect me."

Positive Self-talk

Whenever you do a task well, pat yourself on the back. In this case give yourself some positive self-talk for coming up with solutions and for applying them well, even when you are only mentally rehearsing your interventions. Praising yourself for doing the right thing will help you keep doing it. For example, you might say: "I'm pleased. I turned around and went home. I can control my deviant impulses."

Notice how "Paul Pedophile" used these five steps to rehearse controlling his deviant impulses and become "Paul Prevention":

Paul is my name. One of my risk situations is taking a second look at a young boy because I immediately start fantasizing about the size of his penis.

In treatment I learned about Relapse Rehearsal, so about a month ago I decided to do Relapse Rehearsal about seeing boys I'm attracted to. I've worked on my risk situations before, so I know them pretty well. For this rehearsal I used one of my common problem situations: seeing boys in restaurants. I wanted to use a combination of *avoidance, thought-stopping, self-talk,* and *escape.*

Finding a quiet time is not a problem for me because I live alone, but to make sure I was not interrupted, I unplugged my phone. The night I did this, I was really tired because I'd been working some overtime. So instead of lying down—I thought I might fall asleep—I sat on the couch for my Relapse Rehearsal.

First I relaxed by doing Progressive Relaxation, but instead of starting with my feet, like they taught us, I usually start with my head and work down my body. Then I emptied my mind by saying—well, it's kind of embarrassing to write this, but it means something to me. It's a goal, a kind of affirmation of what I want: "I can and will improve my life today." I say it over and over until my mind is empty.

Then I built up a picture of myself in my favorite restaurant, a pie shop near home. It's a little tacky and plastic, but the food is really good in an old fashioned kind of way. I pictured myself sitting in one of their green vinyl booths, leaning my elbows on the pink formica table with a piece of apple pie with vanilla ice cream and a cup of coffee, black, in front of me. I visualized two 12-year-old boys coming into the restaurant and sitting at the counter directly in my line of vision.

I pictured myself using *avoidance* by immediately turning in my booth so I couldn't look at the boys. But that's not enough, because I'd still be thinking about them, even though I couldn't see them. I saw myself yell, "STOP!" to myself, following it with my rational *self-talk.* In this rehearsal I saw and heard me saying to myself, "These boys are innocent. They don't know I'm a child molester and probably would run away if they found out. I did not choose to get into this situation but I can choose to get out of it." Then I used *escape*, picturing myself leaving the last three bites of pie puddled in melted ice cream, going up to the register to pay my check (the waiters are too slow), paying, and quickly walking out, never once looking at the boys.

When I finished my Relapse Rehearsal, I gave myself a pat on the back: "Good going!" Then I started at the beginning and ran through the whole thing again three or four times. I felt like I really could do it in real life. I've been in the pie shop since my Relapse Rehearsal, but only late at night when kids aren't likely to be there, so I haven't actually had to use it yet. But just knowing I can makes me feel stronger and more in control.

The more you practice Relapse Rehearsal, and the better you are at using your intervention tools, the more effectively you can get back on the right track when you are in a lapse or high-risk situation.

Chapter 11 Assignments

⚭ **Do not write in this workbook** ⚭

46. Write out the details of the five steps of Relapse Rehearsal as they apply to one of your risk situations.

47. Practice Relapse Rehearsal every day for seven days. Keep notes on the results of your experiences. Write down what you have learned about yourself.

Review your answers to these assignments with your therapist and your group. If you are working on your own, share your answers with a friend or person you trust.

12.

Voice Dialogue

VOICE DIALOGUE IS AN ADVANCED FORM of therapy. Its basic principle is that you are made up of many voices, or parts. Your personality has kind parts, selfish parts, deviant parts, generous parts, loving and hating parts, parts that are powerful and parts that are weak. As your situation changes, different parts come out, which is why you do not act the same way all the time. *You are responsible for how you (or any part of you) act.* You also decide which parts of yourself you develop and strengthen, as well as which parts you weaken.

Each part of you acts somewhat differently. How you act with your wife is probably very different from how you act at work or with your best buddy. How you act with your religious fellowship is definitely different from how you acted with your victim. The idea that we have many parts or voices, each of which thinks, feels, speaks, and acts differently, explains why you can be a nice guy one day and a creep the next. For example, consider Dan's case:

My name is Dan. I go to work every day as a clerk in an auto parts store. Tony, my boss, says I'm a "good employee" at work. Sometimes he calls me "Dependable Dan," because I'm on time, patient and polite with customers, and careful with details. I get pretty regular raises and Tony seems to like me.

About a month ago, Tony asked if I'd like to go have a cup of coffee after work with him. I said, "Sure! I'll drive if you buy." So we went. It was the weirdest thing, but Tony, who's no chicken—he chased some punks out of the store with a tire iron last year—was grabbing onto the chicken handle over the passenger door. His knuckles were white. We got to the restaurant, sat down for coffee, and he turns to me and says, "Dan, I swear I'm never going to ride with you again! I'd rather take a cab back to the shop than let you

drive me back. You may be 'Dependable Dan' in the shop, but you're *'Demon Driver Dan'* behind the wheel!"

I thought he was just pulling my leg—there's nothing wrong with my driving. Sure, I've had a few smashups, and if the cops catch me speeding one more time I'll lose my license for sure. They're just trying to make their quota—they figure anybody driving a hot-looking car like mine must be breaking some law. I'm not doing anything wrong.

"Danny," Tony says, "I don't get what's the matter with you. In the store you're really easy to get along with, but you were screaming and cursing that guy driving the red Chevy. You went five blocks out of the way following him when he wouldn't move out of the passing lane. Thank God you don't act like this in the store! You keep driving like that and you'll end up dead or taking the bus permanently when they lift your license."

"Tony," I told him, "what are you talking about? I'm a good driver. Do I look crazy to you? The cops are just down on me because of my flashy car. I'm okay. C'mon, I'll drop you back at the shop." Tony wouldn't get into the car with me. He was acting very strange. I waited with him until his taxi came and then we said goodbye. I don't know what he is talking about. I think maybe he is the one who is crazy.

These are only two out of many parts of Dan's personality. One side of him is tolerant and one is aggressive. In different circumstances different parts come out. The problem is that Dan does not even know about these two sides, Dependable Dan and Demon Driver Dan. He doesn't understand why he gets so many speeding tickets and he may lose his license. Dan thinks he is a nice guy, because *when he is **thinking**, he **is** a nice guy.* When he's not thinking, for instance when he's in "drive mode," Dan is wild and reckless. To change his behavior, keep his license, and lower his insurance rates, Dan needs to become aware of both sides of himself.

For someone dealing with sexual deviancy, a simple way to use these ideas is to think of yourself as having two sides. One side likes deviant sexual behavior, the excitement and sense of power of victimizing someone. Another side likes healthy behavior, having a sense of self-control and responsibility. Each side thinks, feels, and acts differently.

Consider the part of you that is sexually deviant. Your sexually deviant part might think like Dexter, a child molester, or Rick, a rapist:

Dexter's child-molester part thinks:

I really like kids.
I like to play with them.
They are so warm and loving.
They are safe.
They are innocent and pure.
It's okay to be with him, nothing will happen.
I'll just talk to them for a few minutes.
Every man deserves to be around his kids.
If I don't teach her about sex who will?
He is a cutie.
I wonder how well hung he is?

Rick's rapist part thinks:

I'd like to get in her pants.
A few beers with her won't hurt.
Women like men to be strong with them.
When she says no, I'm more interested.
Hey, it's okay to fantasize about forcing her—I wouldn't really do it.
It's okay to watch her undress, she'll never know it.
I love to drive alone at night. It is relaxing, who knows who I might meet.
A man has his needs, a woman should meet them.

These are just a few examples of how your deviant part might talk to you. Your healthy side might talk very differently. It might say something like Dexter's decent part, or Rick's rational part:

Dexter's decent part thinks:

This is a risk situation, get out.
Thinking about kids gets me in trouble.
If I love kids, I'll leave them alone.
Close the door, don't buy anything.
Being around children is not good for me.
I won't sit next to her.
Fantasies about kids lead to trouble.
Giving gifts to kids leads to trouble.
How would my PO see this situation?
Let her mother talk about sex with her, it is not my business.

Rick's rational part thinks:

Women are not sexual objects.
Alcohol will only make my problems worse.
Watching her is not good for me.
Anger and sex don't mix.
When I'm lonely, I'll go to an AA meeting, not a bar.
Get to know her as a person.
When she says no, she means it.
If she knew she'd be terrified.
I'll cool off before I think of sex.

Your sexually deviant side is subtle. When that part of you is in control, you gradually talk yourself into increasingly risky situations and deviant behavior. When you listen to that side of you for long enough, you slowly slide backward. But trying to pretend that your deviant side isn't there any more doesn't work—in fact, pretending lets you be less aware of your behavior and makes you more likely to reoffend. Listening to your healthy side will keep you safe and acting normally. It will protect you and everyone with whom you come in contact. It will help you succeed in life.

The problem is how to know which side you are listening to. They can sound alike. For example, when an inner voice is telling you, "It is okay to love children," is that a healthy part or a deviant part? The answer depends on who you are and what your behavior is like. If you are a child molester, it would be deviant; if you were a good father with a non-deviant adult sex life, it would be healthy.

Using Voice Dialogue

Imagine you have a healthy voice and a deviant voice, each of which has something to say about *every* situation. Learn to hear what both sides have to say: by listening to the deviant side you will understand what it is *bad* to do; by listening to the healthy side you will understand what it is *good* to do. When you try to listen to them one after the other, it will become clear which is which. Consider Ernie's situation:

My name is Ernest, but my friends call me Ernie. I'm a flasher, an exhibitionist. I used to masturbate, drive, and look at women for hours at a time. Whenever I saw the right woman in the right spot, I'd pull the car over and flash at her. Eventually I got caught and got into treatment.

After two years in treatment, I learned about Voice Dialogue and practiced it for months. Whenever I was in a new situation I'd start asking myself, "What would Ernie Exhibitionist want to do now? And what would Ernie Excellent, the healthy part of me, want to do?" I'd listen carefully to each voice and decide what to do.

One day last January I was wearing my long winter coat as I waited at a bus stop. A woman came walking up and then turned, staring out at the street, waiting for a bus just like I was. You know, it was really tempting to set it up so I could start a conversation with her and masturbate under my coat. But then I stopped, like I was supposed to, and asked myself, "What does Ernie Exhibitionist say?" Bad old Ernie Exhibitionist answered, "Look at her all you want, she's beautiful. She must want me to stare at her. You could stand close to her—maybe she will notice you and start a conversation. You'd like to masturbate. She'll never know. In just a few minutes she'll get on the bus. You could expose to her as she leaves. Maybe you could even brush up against her as she gets on the bus."

Then I asked myself what Ernie Excellent, my healthy side, would say. I was a little surprised when Ernie Excellent answered me, "This is a bus stop and you are a strange man. She probably is nervous. Remember you can use *avoidance* now: don't get close to her and don't stare at her. Get your hands out of your pockets and in plain sight. You should just leave, *escape*—this is a high-risk situation. Take a later bus. Go walk around the block." He's a smart fella, that Ernie Excellent. He's kept me out of court and out of trouble!

When his two sides were contrasted in this manner Ernie could decide what was healthy and what was not. Take situations you encounter during the day and write out what your deviant and healthy parts or voices say. In this way you get a better idea about what is deviant and what is healthy.

Chapter 12 Assignments

48. Take a risk situation you encountered recently. Write out what your deviant side would say about it. Be sure to include the thoughts you would think, the behaviors you are tempted to do, and the feelings that your deviant side feels. Then take the same risk situation and write out what your healthy side would think, feel, and do.

49. Write down five of your common risk situations. Then write what your deviant and healthy parts would say about them.

50. Pick one situation during each day for the next week. Write down what your deviant and healthy sides would say about the situation.

Review your answers to these assignments with your therapist and your group. If you are working on your own, share your answers with a friend or person you trust.

13.

Behavioral Contracts

IF YOU ARE IN A TREATMENT PROGRAM, you may have signed a paper saying that you agree to follow certain rules, to behave in certain ways, and to abstain from other behaviors (such as drinking or using drugs). This kind of agreement is also called a contract. When you fulfill your side of the contract, you will get some specified reward, like getting to continue treatment, or getting some privilege. When you break your contract by doing something you agreed not to, you will experience specified consequences, like being dropped from the program or being denied privileges.

This chapter will cover two kinds of contracts: *Lapse Contracts* and *Personal Maintenance Program Contracts*. As you near your transition from an inpatient treatment program to aftercare and self-monitoring, you may be required to prepare a discharge contract that includes a *Lapse Contract*. While making the transition from treatment to self-monitoring, you may be required to develop a *Personal Maintenance Program*. If you are working alone with this workbook, you can make these contracts with yourself and tell at least one other person about them.

Lapse Contracts

A *Lapse Contract* is a formal written agreement you make with your therapist, treatment group, or an important other person. Its purpose is to help you not relapse by encouraging you to be aware of your lapses. In it you specify limits to your behavior and what you will do if you are in a risk situation or lapse into deviant behavior.

Suppose, for example, that masturbating to a deviant fantasy is one of your risk factors. As you know, masturbating to a deviant fantasy is a *lapse* that

sets you up to relapse. Therefore, you would write a Lapse Contract to help you identify, avoid, escape from, and control masturbation. Your Lapse Contract might read as follows:

> I will not masturbate to deviant fantasies. I will make every effort to avoid having deviant fantasies. If I start to have a deviant fantasy I will use thought-stopping or aversive imagery to stop the fantasy. If in bed, I will get out of bed, exercise with 25 situps, and take a cold shower. If I continue to have the fantasy I will avoid masturbating to it by talking to someone and not allowing myself to be alone. If I am successful in controlling the fantasy and not masturbating to it, I will give myself one point. Every time I get 10 points I'll buy some great ice cream as a reward. If I fail to control the fantasy and masturbate, I will tell my wife or womanfriend and my therapist, group, or friend, mark it in my calendar, and subtract 5 points. In addition I will write a one-page report about what I was thinking before I masturbated.

A Lapse Contract such as the one above allows for a variety of interventions. It also provides clear rewards for the intervention and consequences for lapsing.

The Lapse Contract encourages you to use the interventions you have learned until you successfully exit from the risk situation, thus preventing a relapse. Remember, *thoughts can occur in seconds and subsequent behaviors in minutes*. If you don't develop a good Lapse Contract or practice your interventions, you could find yourself relapsing quickly.

Personal Maintenance Program Contracts

A *Personal Maintenance Program Contract* is more extensive than a Lapse Contract. Lapse Contracts cover specific behaviors such as masturbation, using pornography, contact with children, etc. A Personal Maintenance Program Contract covers a variety of areas and issues; it is like a road map for your life.

A Personal Maintenance Program Contract should be flexible enough to be changed, updated, and added to as you learn more about yourself and how you relate to the world. You will want your Personal Maintenance Program Contract to reflect your new understanding.

Below is an outline you can use for developing your Personal Maintenance Program Contract. In each section identify observable behaviors and warning signals. Be sure to note anything indicating you are entering your deviant cycle of behavior, a risk situation, or a lapse.

Preparing Your Personal Maintenance Program Contract

If you have worked through both previous SOS workbooks, you have learned about all the areas discussed in a typical Personal Maintenance Contract. Completing this contract gives you a chance to put all of your work together. Preparing your Personal Maintenance Program Contract will take time, thought, and effort. The document outlined below has been simplified for this workbook, but even so, it could easily be 10 or more typed pages in length. It will be important to share each step of your work with others.

I. Write your **Name** and the **Date** of the contract.
II. **Describe Your Sexual Offense(s).** In this section, describe the details of the types of sexual crimes you have committed, including information in the following three areas:
  1. *Sex and age range of your victims,* for example: boys ages 6 through 9 years; females ages 17 through 37 years.
  2. *Specific sexual acts,* including exactly what you did to your victims, for example: fondle, perform oral sex, masturbate, anal sex, forced intercourse, etc.
  3. *Assault process,* including exactly how you committed your sexual offenses, your thoughts, feelings, and actions. Brief examples:

rape victims at knife point; use a gun; trick or bribe children; tell kids to cooperate or they will get hurt; etc.

III. **Describe Your Deviant Cycle.** In your workbook *Why Did I Do It Again? (SOS Two)* you constructed your deviant cycle in great detail. In this section you will be incorporating information from your deviant cycle into your Personal Maintenance Program Contract.
A. **Describe the beginning of your cycle** with information in the following three areas:
  1. *Thoughts.* Outline the thoughts that occur when you are getting into your cycle and preparing to act out. For example: I think, "What's the use, she's asking for it, no one cares," etc.
  2. *Feelings.* Outline the feelings you experience when you are entering your cycle. For example: "I feel rejected, I feel insecure, I feel angry, I feel inadequate," etc.
  3. *Observable behaviors.* Describe the behaviors you engage in when you are entering your cycle. For example: "I isolate myself from others, I get high on alcohol and drugs, I don't eat properly, I make sexual comments about women/children I see," etc.
B. **Describe the four phases of your deviant cycle:** In SOS Two you developed your deviant cycle and learned about its phases. Write a description of each of the four phases of your deviant cycle.
  1. *Build-up Phase.* List the components of your Build-up Phase. For example: get depressed, look at pornography and masturbate, think irrational thoughts, use alcohol and/or drugs, get angry at home, look for victims, fantasize about future crimes, etc.
  2. *Acting-out Phase.* Describe the crimes you commit and the thinking and feelings that go with them. For example, "I rape teenage girls between the ages of 14 and

17 at gunpoint. I force them to have oral sex with me. When I do this I feel powerful and strong. I think, 'I can make them do anything I want.' I think of them as my sexual slaves."

"I molest girls and boys between the ages of 7 and 10. I perform oral sex on them and make them masturbate me. When I do these things, I fulfill a twisted desire I have. When I complete an act I feel powerful and competent because I have been able to trick the children into giving me what I want."

3. *Justification Phase.* Describe the thoughts, feelings, and behaviors you use to justify your crimes during the Acting-out Phase. For example, "I didn't hurt them. I was just teaching them about sex. She'll get over it. I will never do this again. He really wanted it. I denied all my emotions. I told the kids I would go to jail if they talked. I told the kids it would kill their mother if she found out," etc.

4. *Pretend-normal Phase.* List the types of things you do, think, and feel to cover up your problems and give the appearance that your life is okay. For example: "I'm extra nice to my family. I work hard at my job. I will never look at pornography and will get rid of any pornography I own. I cut back on my drinking," etc.

C. **Describe How Your Deviant Cycle Affects Your Life:** Your deviant cycle affects all areas of your life. Each area will have normal behaviors and deviant behaviors. Explain both normal and deviant behaviors for the following:

1. *Social Life.* Your social life refers to your relationships with family and friends. How do those relationships change as you go into your deviant cycle? For example, "I stop going out socially. I turn down invitations from my friends. I close them out of my life. I withdraw from my family. I don't let them know what is going on."

2. *Work.* Describe how your behavior at work changes as you enter the Build-up Phase. For example: "I skip days from work. I get to work late or leave early. I get high on the job," etc.

3. *School.* If you go to school, describe how your school performance changes when you enter the Build-up Phase. For example: "I cut classes, my grades go down, I drop out of school," etc.

4. *Home.* Describe how your home life changes because of entering the Build-up Phase. For example: "I get sloppy. I don't put things away. I get angry with my wife. I withhold sex from my partner," etc.

5. *Sleep.* Describe how your sleeping pattern changes as you enter the Build-up Phase. For example: "I go to sleep very early or very late. I don't sleep as much as usual. I sleep more than usual. I stay up all night and sleep all day," etc.

6. *Hunger and Appetite.* Describe how your eating patterns change. For example: "I eat junk food. I eat more than usual. I drink two quarts of coffee a day. I skip meals," etc.

7. *Appearance.* Describe how your appearance and grooming change. For example: "I don't shave. I look tired. I lose weight. My hair gets long and unkempt. I dress up to look sharp only when I go out cruising," etc.

8. *Finances.* Detail what you do with your money as you enter the Build-up Phase. For example: "I spend money foolishly. I don't pay my bills. I start gambling. I buy kids presents. I blow my money on alcohol, drugs, pornography," etc.

9. *Alcohol and Drugs.* Describe your use of alcohol and drugs. For example: "I increase my drinking to two six-packs a day. I drink anything I can get my hands on. I smoke three ounces of pot a week. I use speed and downers. I start on a meth run," etc.

10. *Driving.* It is likely that your driving habits change if your car is a part of your deviancy. Describe how your driving habits change if you use your car to look for victims, to search for places where your assault can take place, or to assault your victims in. For example, "I drive around for hours cruising for victims. I take my car to the park. I get my car ready so I can have sex with kids in it. I stock my car with rope and blankets. I buy kids' toys to keep in the car," etc.

11. *Other areas of life not specified above.*

IV. **Special Environmental Restrictions.** In setting up your Personal Maintenance Program Contract give yourself the best possible chances of succeeding by placing certain environmental restrictions on yourself. For example, if you should not be around children, your contract should state: "I must live in a neighborhood primarily of adults." If you should not be around teenage females, your contract should state: "I will not work near a high school or at a job that caters to teenagers." If you have a drinking problem, your contract should state: "I will not have alcohol in my home." Review the list of special conditions in Chapter Three. Select the ones that apply to you and enter them in your Personal Maintenance Program Contract.

V. **Interventions.** Write detailed interventions for each stage of your deviant cycle. You should have several alternative ways of handling each problem. Consider the specific thoughts and actions you will use to intervene. This should be the most extensive part of your Personal Maintenance Program Contract.

VI. **Positive Self-enhancing Activities.** Besides eliminating unhealthy behaviors, your contract will include positive, healthy activities to enhance your self-esteem and help you handle stress more effectively. For example, "I will join a club that has weekly meetings. I will attend AA and NA meetings every day. I will go out for coffee with a friend four times a week. I will exercise three times a week at the local YMCA during low-risk times. I will go bowling once a week. I will take vitamins regularly and eat three meals a day," etc. Be sure to specify how often you will participate in positive activities.

VII. **Long-term goals.** Describe what you hope to achieve in the next 6 months, 12 months, 2 years, and 5 years.

A Personal Maintenance Program Contract is a complex plan for your life. It is important to think it through thoroughly before you end therapy. Developing a contract with the guidance of a therapist is the best way to ensure your plan is complete and realistic. However, working on your own with someone you trust, who knows about your deviancy, can be a helpful way to plan for your maintenance and growth.

This task is not an easy one. When you have completed it, you will have many pages of solid plans to show for your efforts. This is one of the most important tasks you will do in therapy. The results are what you will take with you as you make the transition into aftercare and self-monitoring. It will be a concrete expression of all the hard work you have done.

Chapter 13 Assignment

51. Following the outline in this chapter, write out the details of your Personal Maintenance Program Contract.

Review your answer to this assignment with your therapist and your group. If you are working on your own, share your answer with a friend or person you trust.

14.

Monitoring Myself Through Journaling

FOR YOU, AS FOR MOST SEX OFFENDERS, one of the most difficult parts of breaking your deviant cycle is recognizing when you are in it. Keeping a notebook where you write down day-to-day events and your reactions to them is an effective way to observe yourself and your cycle. After several weeks, your journal entries will show your patterns of behavior. By noticing unhealthy patterns earlier and earlier you will be able to identify ways to change them more quickly. Your journal can be a valuable tool for keeping yourself on track.

The journal technique is a way of keeping track of your life's events and learning how they influence you. The journal is set up to help you understand the difference between *events* and *your reactions* to them. "Events" are all the large and small things that happen around you and to you. A large event could be getting fired from a job. A small event could be a brief conversation at breakfast. Any event, large or small, could trigger thoughts and feelings that you could use to start your deviant cycle. By writing about events and your reactions to them, you will learn about making choices for better ways of thinking, feeling, and acting.

Try this experiment:

1. Think back through the past couple of days. List in your notebook three or four interactions you have had with your wife, co-workers, or people you talked to.
2. Ask yourself, "What feelings, thoughts, or behaviors did I have during and after these events?"
3. Next, think about recent times when you have been alone and list three or four in your notebook. Remember what you were feeling then and write it down. Perhaps you were bored or restless. Maybe you had strong feelings about something you read

in the newspaper, or thoughts about something you saw on TV. These are the small (and maybe not so small) events and reactions that will make up the bulk of your journal.

If you keep track of several events every day, they will provide you with information you can use to discover ways your behavior repeats or forms a pattern. Seeing your patterns will help you quickly see your unhealthy behavior, predict where it would lead, and intervene appropriately.

Writing In Your Journal

Monitoring yourself with the journal process begins with three steps: (1) keeping notes, (2) setting aside time, and (3) laying out the page.

Keeping notes.

The purpose of a self-monitoring journal is to help you recognize which events trigger unhealthy feelings, thoughts, and behaviors. The first step in doing this is to keep notes. Carry a 3x5 index card in your pocket during the day. As things happen, make a note on the card to remind yourself of the incident later. Make a note about the events you have a strong reaction to and think about several times later in the day. The note may be as brief as naming the people involved and the time. Or you may choose to jot down a few words to describe the incident. Later on you will use these notes to write more complete entries in your journal.

For instance, suppose an event was getting caught in traffic on your way to work. You could take a moment to make a reminder note on your card. The words "late for work—stressed" would be all you need to remember the event at the end of the day.

Setting aside time.

Setting aside a daily time to make journal entries is an important part of monitoring yourself. Without a regular time to sit down with your journal each day, you will quickly forget the whole thing. If you don't take time daily, you may overlook the small incidents that happen repeatedly while you wait for the big ones that "really matter." But it is often the small incidents that teach you the most about yourself. These small incidents give you the most information about the early steps in your deviant cycle that are the easiest to change. Most offenders find that by the time the large, more serious events happen, many relevant but smaller ones have gone by unnoticed.

Laying out the page.

Use lined paper with holes for collecting pages in a three-ring binder, or write in an 8½ x 11 or larger spiral notebook. Begin by drawing a vertical line down the middle of the page. Write the date of the incident and the approximate time it happened on the first line, on the left side. Now, writing only to the left of the vertical line, write down the first event you have decided to record. Give enough information to be able to reread the entry six weeks from now and make sense of what happened.

Chas, a child molester, is learning how to keep a journal. His first page looked like this:

EVENTS	REACTIONS
8 am. Jan [his wife] asked me to come home early today to take the cat to the vet. She complained that it was my turn because she thinks I don't do as much of the work taking care of it as she does.	
Lunch time. Had lunch with some of the guys from the plant. While we were there, some kids came by throwing a Frisbee.	
8 pm. Came home early and took the cat to the vet. Got back to the house after dark. Missed the news on TV.	

Like everyone else, Chas had many small events happen during his day. He chose to record these three because he had strong reactions to them. His reactions led him to make either appropriate choices that kept him safe or inappropriate choices that put him at risk of lapsing. Other links we will cover are *thoughts* about the event, *feelings* during the event, *body sensations* while it was happening, *fantasies* during or afterwards, *planning* afterwards, and resulting *behaviors*.

Your journal will allow you to identify and understand each of these steps. Gradually you will be able to see the reactions that encourage your unhealthy behavior and the choices that lead to healthy behavior. Choosing healthy behavior does not depend on what happens to you, but is under your control.

When you understand what you do to shape your behavior, you will have some real choices about how to act instead of react.

Chapter 14 Assignment

∽ **Do not write in this workbook** ∾

52. Divide a page down the middle with a vertical line. *Each day* enter at least three of the day's events in your journal. Start with the most memorable or irritating events. For each event, write down the date, time, and who (if anyone) was with you.

15.
Journaling My Thoughts, Body Sensations, & Feelings

BY NOW YOU SHOULD HAVE A SERIES OF EVENTS WRITTEN in your journal. Look over your entries and ask yourself, "What thoughts was I thinking as each event happened?" Be honest with yourself. Like most people, you probably had many different thoughts, and some may seem to contradict others. For example, suppose one of your events was disagreeing with your womanfriend. You might have thoughts about loving her and in the next moment think about getting even with her. Whatever your thoughts were, write them down.

Look below at Chas's journal. On the right hand side, opposite his description of the events, he wrote his thoughts during each event. It probably seemed to him that some of the thoughts didn't fit together. But they were all real.

Note: All of your thoughts that you report honestly are *real thoughts*. But some of your real thoughts may not be *true*, that is, accurate pictures of what's happening.

Not all of Chas's real thoughts were accurate— some expressed thinking defects. For instance, Chas thought his wife was looking for a fight. But because he was *imagining* what his wife was thinking, Chas's thinking was a distortion of clear thought—a thinking defect.

Journaling Thinking Defects

Thinking defects are thoughts that are *not true*, but which you choose to *believe* are true so that you can justify your unhealthy feelings. They keep you reacting badly to events, keeping you in your deviant cycle. When you choose to believe your distorted thinking, you are choosing to strengthen your deviant behaviors. Your thinking defects feed your deviant cycle to produce your deviant behavior.

Because defective thinking is so much a part of your deviant cycle, it is important for you to observe all your thoughts. After each event, write your thoughts in your journal, then analyze them to see which thoughts are defective and which are not. You will begin to recognize the conditions in which you are most likely to use defective thinking. By reviewing your journal over a long time you will learn how your distorted thoughts lead to your unhealthy feelings and behaviors.

In order to learn to recognize your thinking defects, write down your thoughts to the right of the vertical line. Then go back and ask yourself which thoughts might be distortions. Underline these distorted thoughts, as Chas did in his journal.

EVENTS	REACTIONS
8 am. Jan asked me to come home early today to take the cat to the vet. She complained that it was my turn because she thinks I don't do as much of the work taking care of it as she does.	Thoughts: There she goes again. <u>She's only on my case because she's in a bad mood. She just wants me to feel guilty.</u>

EVENTS	REACTIONS
Lunch time. Had lunch with some of the guys from the plant. While we were there, some kids came by throwing a Frisbee.	Thoughts: Man, those kids are really cute. <u>I bet they would like a grown up to play with them. The little red head over there looks like she's coming on to me.</u> Wait a minute, that's dangerous thinking. I'd better get out of here. This isn't a healthy place for me to be hanging out. I hope no one ribs me about leaving.
8 pm. Came home early and took the cat to the vet. Got back to the house after dark. Missed the news on TV.	Thoughts: I'm really tired of having to bother with the cat. <u>Jan never does anything for it. Nothing ever goes right for me. No one in this family appreciates me.</u>

Notice that Chas's thoughts about the event were different from the actual event. On the left side of the page he recorded what was actually said. Then on the right, he wrote his thoughts about what was said.

Chas underlined some real but inaccurate thoughts, for example, "Jan never does anything for it." This thought was real but probably is not true. It is likely that Jan feeds the cat some of the time, gives it love, lets it outdoors, or buys cat food for it. Chas underlined this thought because it is not accurate.

Someone else talking to Jan about the cat might have thought, "Jan sounds a little angry. I guess we need to talk more about this." Or, "What's the big deal? Let's not fight over something so small," or "I can't leave work early either. I'd better tell Jan." None of these thoughts are distortions, and if Chas had had these thoughts, he would not have underlined them.

Chas's other distortions are at the center of his deviant cycle. When he thinks, "Nothing ever goes right for me," or "No one in this family appreciates me," he is using negative self-talk to feed his self-pity and anger. Eventually he may use those feelings to justify his deviant fantasies and to act out against other people. If he can identify these thoughts as distortions, he can change them and break the feeling links in his deviant cycle.

Review the list of "thinking defects" on pages 21 and 22 in your SOS Two workbook to help you recognize your distortions. The more attention you pay to the difference between defective thinking and healthy thinking, the easier it is to stop using thinking defects. With practice you will learn to identify defective thoughts even before you enter them in your journal. After you have filled in several pages of your notebook, ask a close friend, your therapist, or group members to review your thinking. They may help pick out thinking defects you might have missed.

Chapter 15 Assignments

~ **Do not write in this workbook** ~

53. Continue to enter each day's events in your notebook. Be sure to enter *at least three events **every day*** (remember to leave plenty of room on the page since you will be writing many things in the space opposite the events). On the right side of the page, opposite each event, write the *thoughts* you had while the event was happening. Be honest; write down your *real* thoughts. You may feel embarrassed to record thoughts that you know are distortions, but don't let your embarrassment or hopes of looking good keep you from writing them down. This journal is for you. If you find that you can only remember a few thoughts from the event, ask yourself some questions, and note the answers: for example, "Was I wishing to get away from what was happening? Was I thinking things shouldn't happen like this? Was I having thoughts about 'getting back' at someone?"

54. In your notebook, underline your distorted thoughts.

Journaling Your Body Sensations

When you react to an event, part of your reaction is physical. Body feelings are signals that can help you recognize your emotions. There are many types of *body sensations*, but they are pretty consistent for any one person from situation to situation. For example, how your body reacts when you are angry will be the same regardless of what makes you angry. When you recognize that your body is reacting, ask yourself, "What is my body telling me?" For example, when you notice that your forehead is tight, your jaw is clenched, and your eyes are narrowed, these signs may show that you are feeling critical. When you notice that your shoulders are tense, your jaw is thrust forward, and your hands are clenched, you might think, "Usually my body feels like this when I'm angry. Am I angry now?"

Criticism and anger are not the only emotions that your body reacts to. When you pay attention to what your body is telling you, you can learn to recognize fear, anxiety, boredom, sadness, peace, happiness, security, etc. In fact, your body probably has its own way of translating each emotion you feel. Recording your body sensations in your daily journal will give you practice in recognizing how your body reacts and the emotions those reactions represent.

You can see below how Chas recorded his body sensations.

EVENTS

8 am. Jan asked me to come home early today to take the cat to the vet. She complained that it was my turn because she thinks I don't do as much of the work taking care of it as she does.

REACTIONS

Thoughts: There she goes again. She's only on my case because she's in a bad mood. She just wants me to feel guilty.

Body sensations: Knot in my stomach, tight throat, face flushed, shoulders tense.

EVENTS	REACTIONS
Lunchtime. Had lunch with some of the guys from the plant. While we were there, some kids came by throwing a Frisbee.	**Thoughts:** Man, those kids are really cute. <u>I bet they would like a grown up to play with them.</u> <u>The little red head over there looks like she's coming on to me.</u> Wait a minute, that's dangerous thinking. I'd better get out of here. This isn't a healthy place for me to be hanging out. I hope no one ribs me about leaving. **Body sensations:** Restless, sexually excited, headache, face red.
8 pm. Came home early and took the cat to the vet. Got back to the house after dark. Missed the news on TV.	**Thoughts:** I'm really tired of having to bother with the cat. <u>Jan never does anything for it.</u> <u>Nothing ever goes right for me.</u> <u>No one in this family appreciates me.</u> **Body sensations:** Tense all over, especially in my shoulders and neck; tired; hands jittery; hard to sit still.

If Chas is used to ignoring his emotions, it may be hard for him to recognize when he's angry. If he grew up in a family where it wasn't okay for people to feel angry, he may have an especially difficult time naming his feeling accurately. The same thing is true for other emotions, like sadness or fear. Once Chas has taught himself to pay attention to his body sensations, they will tell him what he's feeling.

Chapter 15 Assignments *(continued)*
∽ Do not write in this workbook ∽

55. From now on, add a section for body sensations to your journal pages. For every event record your body sensations. At first keep a small note pad handy throughout the day so you can make notes to yourself about your body sensations. After you get used to watching for them, you will more easily be able to remember them until you are ready to make your journal entries.

56. On a separate page, list all the body sensations you were aware of for each event. Next to each, write the emotion that went with it. **Keep this list!** It will help you with the next step in the journaling process.

57. Continue your journal, now always adding a *Body Sensations* section for each event.

Journaling Your Feelings

The next step in journal keeping involves identifying and recording the *feelings* you had during the events you wrote down. Writing down your feelings will help clarify them. You will then understand how feelings feed your defective thoughts and keep your deviant cycle going.

Everyone has feelings of fear, loneliness, and shame at one time or another (review the discussion on these feelings in Chapter Four of SOS Two). Because feelings are so uncomfortable, some people deal with them by "stuffing" them. "Stuffing" means trying to get rid of a feeling by pretending it isn't there. Stuffing doesn't make the feeling go away, you're only pushing it out of your awareness. The feeling is still inside but at a deeper level. When you are unaware of what you feel, gradually the feeling begins to control you. Healthy people, in contrast, can control and appropriately express their feelings.

Feelings Feed Thoughts, Thoughts Feed Feelings

Another reason to write your feelings in your journal is that feelings and thoughts feed each other. Often you will have a brief feeling, like mild irritation. This small feeling may be followed by a thought, like, "He's an ass." The thought makes the feeling stronger. Now it is not just mild irritation but anger, leading to angry thoughts, like, "I'll show him ..." As you bounce between your feelings and thoughts you can very quickly become enraged. The more journal work

you do, the more you understand how what you feel is related to what you think. Eventually you will find that by observing and changing your thoughts you will actually make yourself feel differently.

Don't be surprised if you find that for the same incident there are contradictory feelings, just as there may have been contradictory thoughts. You may have had one set of feelings at the beginning of the incident and a different set by the time it was over.

Now look again at the events you recorded in Assignment #53. Think about the feelings and thoughts associated with them. You will probably find that every thought has a feeling associated with it. Likewise, each feeling led to one or more thoughts. The more completely you've written them down, the more you will see the connection between the two.

You Can Change Your Feelings

You can't control whether you have particular feelings, but you can change one feeling into another by changing how you think about events in your life. When you clean up your thinking defects you can avoid many of the "poor me" and "tough guy" feelings that keep your deviant cycle going. Thinking defects make you feel powerless and victimized. When you feel powerless and victimized, you distort your thinking. Before you know it, you're in your deviant cycle.

When Chas added the *Feelings* section to his journal it looked like this:

EVENTS	REACTIONS
8 am. Jan asked me to come home early today to take the cat to the vet. She complained that it was my turn because she thinks I don't do as much of the work taking care of it as she does.	Thoughts: There she goes again. She's only on my case because she's in a bad mood. She just wants me to feel guilty. Body sensations: Knot in my stomach, tight throat, face flushed, shoulders tense.

EVENTS	REACTIONS
	Feelings: Surprised, angry, judged, defensive, resentful.
Lunchtime. Had lunch with some of the guys from the plant. While we were there, some kids came by throwing a Frisbee.	Thoughts: Man, those kids are really cute. <u>I bet they would like a grown up to play with them. The little red head over there looks like she's coming on to me.</u> Wait a minute, that's dangerous thinking. I'd better get out of here. This isn't a healthy place for me to be hanging out. I hope no one ribs me about leaving.
	Body sensations: Restless, sexually excited, headache, face red.
	Feelings: Excited, surprised, playful, aroused, anxious, scared, embarrased.
8 pm. Came home early and took the cat to the vet. Got back to the house after dark. Missed the news on TV.	Thoughts: I'm really tired of having to bother with the cat. <u>Jan never does anything for it. Nothing ever goes right for me. No one in this family appreciates me.</u>
	Body sensations: Tense all over, especially in my shoulders and neck; tired; hands jittery; hard to sit still.
	Feelings: Resentful, angry, revengeful, frustrated, selfish.

It's hard to say which happens first—feelings or thoughts. Whichever it is, deliberately changing your thoughts will change your feelings. It is not as difficult as it may seem. First, recognize when your thoughts are distorted. Then change your unhealthy thinking to healthy thinking. Your feelings will change as your thoughts do.

You may already have a sense of how your distorted thoughts and feelings are connected. As you write in your journal, these patterns will become still more obvious to you.

Each day, continue journaling at least three events and the *thoughts* associated with them. Underline your *thinking defects* in the entry. In the right column, write down the *feelings* you had during each incident.

Chapter 15 Assignments *(continued)*
Do not write in this workbook

58. Look at the relationship between your thoughts and feelings. Each thought should have feelings connected with it, and vice versa. For example, if you think, "That's unfair!" some feeling will accompany it, perhaps resentment. Look back at the list of feelings associated with body sensations in Assignment #56 if you need help. Discuss with your group, therapist, or a close friend the connection between the thinking defects in your journal and the feelings you had. Identify how your distorted thinking fed your feelings and vice versa. Continue keeping a journal each day, including a section for feelings.

It will be helpful to your treatment if you share your answers to these assignments with your therapist and your group. If you are working on your own, share your answers with a friend or person you trust.

16.
Journaling
My Fantasies & Plans

A *FANTASY IS LIKE A DAYDREAM*; it happens when you wonder, "What if ..." or wish for something different to happen than what is happening right now. The "something different" may be a memory from the past or a future event that exists only in your mind.

Your fantasies result from your feelings and thoughts. Although everyone has fantasies, you may find that identifying them is a difficult part of journal writing. Because fantasies are inside your mind, and because you aren't used to talking about them, they can be hard to recognize. Sometimes it is hard to notice that a fantasy is happening, especially if you fantasize often. If you fantasize often you may need the help of a therapist or trusted friend to sort out what is real and what is fantasy.

Another reason fantasies are difficult to journal is that they are extremely private. They make up a part of your deviant cycle that no one knows about unless you choose to tell them. You already know from reading your SOS One and Two workbooks that fantasies are crucial links in your deviant cycle. Writing them in your journal is a major opportunity to show how serious you are about breaking the links of your cycle. All offenders have deviant fantasies. They may be sexual or nonsexual; fantasies of revenge are as unhealthy as deviant sexual fantasies. Acknowledging your deviant fantasies is an essential step for you to gain control over your deviant cycle. Otherwise your fantasy will continue to feed your cycle and you will repeat your sexual crimes.

Why Journal Fantasies?

There are important reasons for adding your fantasies to your journal:

- Journaling fantasies requires you to ask yourself questions about the content of the fantasy. Writing them down will make you more and more aware of what kinds of fantasies they are.
- When you add your fantasies to your journal, you will begin to recognize the events that trigger them.
- Journaling the fantasy is a way of interrupting the cycle the fantasy feeds. In doing so, you will be training yourself to be in control of your cycle.
- Your journal will become a record of the feelings and thoughts most likely to lead to deviant fantasies. You will probably see that you often use your deviant fantasies to protect yourself from difficult and painful emotions like rejection, anger, sadness, or guilt. You use your deviant fantasies to make you feel better temporarily in the same way that you might distract yourself from these feelings by watching TV. They give you a sense of control that helps you forget that your life isn't necessarily going the way you would like. Unfortunately, the sense of control that comes from fantasies is dangerous for sex offenders because it leads to seeking sexual control over others.

Visual Fantasies

Fantasies can take many forms. *Visual* fantasy, a common form, is like a private movie where the screen is inside your head, similar to the screen you used for relaxing with visual imagery (Chapter Nine). One type of visual fantasy is like a daydream: you make up the story and direct all of the actors. You may have a part in the movie or you may be in the audience.

Another type of visual fantasy may be a memory of something that has happened. In this case you remember a past event and replay it over and over again in your mind. With either type the fantasy may be long enough to tell a story or as short as a single picture or a flash of a scene. A short fantasy may be a look of surprise on the face of a victim from your past.

Or it may be a quick mental image of someone naked. Consider Pierre Pedophile's fantasies:

I am Pierre, and my victims have been 8- to 10-year-old boys. When I first began treatment it was very hard for me to understand what fantasies are. First I thought fantasies were always like full-length movies in someone's mind, and I didn't think I had any of those. But then I started learning about my patterns, and I began to realize that I did have fantasies, they just came in different shapes and sizes. Sometimes I'd have a quick snapshot in my mind about how my college roommate's 9-year-old brother might look. When I'd think about this picture, I'd usually fantasize about inviting a boy over to watch X-rated videos so I could have sex with him.

Sometimes I'd fantasize about something that really happened. For instance, before I started treatment, I'd remember molesting Adam, my first victim. Usually I would relive the memory, feel very aroused, and masturbate to my memory-fantasy.

Both of Pierre's ways of seeing images are fantasies, one remembered and one made up. Pierre uses both types of fantasy to feed his deviant thoughts and perhaps to set himself up to reoffend; therefore, both are dangerous for him. He can stop both, but first he has to train himself to recognize that he is having them.

Writing them down is an effective way of tuning in to what's going on in his fantasy life.

Recording Your Fantasies

Chas had written in his journal three different events that might have triggered fantasies. He recorded his fantasies about the events like this:

EVENTS	REACTIONS
8 am. Jan asked me to come home early today to take the cat to the vet. She complained that it was my turn because she thinks I don't do as much of the work taking care of it as she does.	**Thoughts:** There she goes again. She's only on my case because she's in a bad mood. She just wants me to feel guilty. **Body sensations:** Knot in my stomach, tight throat, face flushed, shoulders tense. **Feelings:** Surprised, angry, judged, defensive, resentful. **Fantasies:** Saying no and stomping out of the house. Not going home at all after work. Jan wondering where I was.

EVENTS	REACTIONS
Lunchtime. Had lunch with some of the guys from the plant. While we were there, some kids came by throwing a Frisbee.	Thoughts: Man, those kids are really cute. <u>I bet they would like a grown up to play with them. The little red head over there looks like she's coming on to me.</u> Wait a minute, that's dangerous thinking. I'd better get out of here. This isn't a healthy place for me to be hanging out. I hope no one ribs me about leaving.
	Body sensations: Restless, sexually excited, headache, face red.
	Feelings: Excited, surprised, playful, aroused, anxious, scared, embarrased.
	Fantasies: Playing frisbee with the children. Walking off with one of the children.
8pm. Came home early and took the cat to the vet. Got back to the house after dark. Missed the news on TV.	Thoughts: I'm really tired of having to bother with the cat. <u>Jan never does anything for it. Nothing ever goes right for me. No one in this family appreciates me.</u>
	Body sensations: Tense all over, especially in my shoulders and neck; tired; hands jittery; hard to sit still.
	Feelings: Resentful, angry, revengeful, frustrated, selfish.
	Fantasies: Not going home. Killing the cat. Telling Jan off. Later: walking in woods with one of the children I saw at lunch time.

Notice how Chas's anger led him into two different kinds of fantasies. He first fantasized about really showing his anger to his wife. At midday he fantasized about the children, fantasies that, if not interrupted, would have developed into fantasies of deviant sex. Fortunately he had trained himself to recognize that his deviant fantasies start with images of being with children, and he stopped them early enough to decide to leave the situation.

Later at night, when he was again mad at his wife, at first he had fantasies of venting his anger at his wife on the cat. But then he noticed himself fantasizing about children. Because he was used to writing down these experiences as they happened, he realized quickly that he was in the beginning of a lapse. He stopped the fantasy and ended the lapse.

Chapter 16 Assignments

 **Do not write in this workbook**

59. Starting with today's journal entry, write down the *fantasies* that are part of each day's events. Pay special attention to how one fantasy may lead into another.

60. Write down the kinds of fantasies that come with various emotions. What thoughts seem to keep the fantasy going? What thoughts stop it? Continue to record your other reactions (thoughts, feelings, body sensations) as well.

Journaling Your Plans

As you have learned from your work in your SOS One and Two workbooks, deviant behavior does not "just happen." In reality, your behavior usually begins with thoughts, feelings, and sometimes fantasies. Then you think about how it would be if the fantasies came true. You begin to plan or mentally rehearse how to act it out. *Planning* is what connects your deviant thoughts, feelings, and fantasies with your dangerous behavior. You *plan* how you move from what is going on inside your mind to acting it out.

You plan for many kinds of behavior, not just sexual deviance. There is positive planning as well as negative planning. If you have fantasies of getting a raise, you may move from the fantasies to considering how to get the raise by planning to work longer hours or to speak to the boss. Whatever the fantasy, planning makes it happen. The planning is the step during which you get ready to act out the fantasy. Planning

always involves decisions. Your planning is your way of moving your attention from what is going on in your head to what you are going to do about it.

Planning is also present when you behave habitually. Habits are the results of plans that have been acted on many times. Though your actions happen one step at a time, each step requires a decision, even when the action is repeated frequently. These habits can be broken by examining and journaling what specific plans follow each of your fantasies.

It is important to understand the difference between your fantasies and your plans. *When you are aware of moving from fantasizing to planning, you will understand how to stay in control of your behavior.* Sometimes they may seem so connected it is difficult to tell where fantasies end and planning begins. Practice is the solution here—practice and sharing with someone who is following your treatment. Look at Chas's "planning" journal entries.

EVENTS	REACTIONS
8 am. Jan asked me to come home early today to take the cat to the vet. She complained that it was my turn because she thinks I don't do as much of the work taking care of it as she does.	**Thoughts:** There she goes again. She's only on my case because she's in a bad mood. She just wants me to feel guilty.
	Body sensations: Knot in my stomach, tight throat, face flushed, shoulders tense.
	Feelings: Surprised, angry, judged, defensive, resentful.
	Fantasies: Saying no and stomping out of the house. Not going home at all after work. Jan wondering where I was.
	Planning: Tell Jan how angry I am later. Stop at the diner for a more peaceful breakfast before work.
Lunchtime. Had lunch with some of the guys from the plant. While we were there, some kids came by throwing a Frisbee.	**Thoughts:** Man, those kids are really cute. I bet they would like a grown up to play with them. The little red head over there looks like she's coming on to me. Wait a minute, that's dangerous thinking. I'd better get out of here. This isn't a healthy place for me to be hanging out. I hope no one ribs me about leaving.
	Body sensations: Restless, sexually excited, headache, face red.
	Feelings: Excited, surprised, playful, aroused, anxious, scared, embarrased.
	Fantasies: Playing frisbee with the children. Walking off with one of the children.

EVENTS	REACTIONS
8 pm. Came home early and took the cat to the vet. Got back to the house after dark. Missed the news on TV.	**Planning:** Stay away from this park in the future. Find someone to talk to about this event. Later, when I'm calmer, tell the guys why I left so quickly.

Thoughts: I'm really tired of having to bother with the cat. <u>Jan never does anything for it. Nothing ever goes right for me. No one in this family appreciates me.</u>

Body sensations: Tense all over, especially in my shoulders and neck; tired; hands jittery; hard to sit still.

Feelings: Resentful, angry, revengeful, frustrated, selfish.

Fantasies: Not going home. Killing the cat. Telling Jan off. Later: walking in woods with one of the children I saw at lunch time.

Planning: Talk to Jan and tell how upset I was this morning. Tell her about the fantasies. |

If Chas were not so committed to getting control over his deviant thoughts and behaviors, he might have planned not to return home after work. Or, later, he might have planned to go back to the park to see the children. If he had made these plans and entered them in his journal, Chas would realize he was in a high-risk situation and was lapsing. The journal would have helped him see he was beginning to act on his fantasies. The fact Chas has begun to plan does not mean he will necessarily carry it out. He can change his planning at any time.

Chapter 16 Assignments *(continued)*

61. Add a planning section to today's journal entries. Underline the planning or decisions that moved you closer to acting on your deviant fantasies. This planning brings you closer to reoffending. Ask yourself, "Are these plans I've written my real plans when the event was happening?"

62. Write out in what way your plans move you into, take you out of, or keep you in a lapse. If you follow through on your plans, will you be more likely or less likely to reoffend?

63. Continue writing at least three journal entries a day, including thoughts, distortions, body sensations, feelings, fantasies, and planning for each event.

It would be helpful to your treatment if you shared your answers to these assignments with your therapist and your group. If you are working on your own, share your answers with a friend or person you trust.

17.
Recognizing My Behavior Patterns Through Journaling

YOU HAVE LEARNED A LOT about keeping a journal. You know that even the small events in your day can teach you about yourself and how you react. You are learning how to recognize what you are feeling when events happen. You know which body sensations signal particular emotions and which thoughts feed those emotions. By now you also should be getting better at picking out which thoughts are distortions.

You can also begin to see which events, feelings, and thoughts are most likely to trigger deviant sexual fantasies. You are beginning to recognize when your fantasies lead to negative planning, and finally, how you either act on or interrupt your planning. Identifying each of these separate reactions to an event will become easier the longer you keep your journal.

The patterns you are working to change are the repetitions that define your unhealthy behavior. To get a clear sense of your own patterns, you will need to reread your journal entries from the last several weeks. Being able to review periods of your life is one reason for recording events *every* day.

One of the patterns you can discover from your journal is that the negative events and reactions, the ones that don't feel good, are the very ones you repeat. Even though they may feel awful, they hold some appeal—otherwise you wouldn't be repeating them so consistently. These *negative payoffs* are the feelings that allow you to move along in your deviant cycle.

Consider how Robin Righteous used his payoff to continue his deviant behavior:

> **My name is Robin.** I used to think that when things didn't go my way, the only thing I could do was feel bad or stupid. When I felt bad or inadequate, I thought other people were being unfair to me and I resented it. As I was rereading my journal entries over the past few weeks, I realized something pretty startling: *my own decisions were encouraging people to be critical of me!* What surprised me the most was realizing that these negative decisions and actions gave me a kind of payoff: when people criticized me, I got to feel lonely and inadequate, and then feel that I was *unfairly wronged.* My reward, my payoff, was that feeling of being "unfairly wronged." It was clear from what I'd underlined in my journal that I was using my distorted thoughts to stay in these feelings. Whenever I felt unfairly wronged, I was using those feelings to justify having my deviant thoughts and fantasies. I had been telling myself, "Well, if everyone is going to be so unfair to me, I have a right to take care of myself with these fantasies."

Anger, self-pity, self-righteousness, confusion, and other negative emotions can be used as payoffs to distort thinking and justify deviant behavior. These feelings can be payoffs because they allow you to feel you deserve to be able to do some deviant activity.

Your payoff patterns will show up as you track how your feelings tend to worsen with events. You may tend to go from feeling lonely (at the beginning of an event) into feeling angry and then justified and self-righteous. Or perhaps you begin by feeling angry and, through distortions, move yourself into feeling sad and rejected. Frequently the payoff feeling leads directly to falsely justified deviant fantasies. When you do not make the choice to stop them, your deviant fantasies become plans and eventually you relapse.

Careful reading of past entries will help you uncover your own patterns. Sharing them with someone participating in your treatment is a vital part of understanding them.

By doing the exercises that follow, you will uncover several different patterns in your journal entries. The process will help you continue to learn more about yourself and your behavior chains. And the more you know about your patterns, the more power you will have to change them.

Chapter 17 Assignment

 Do not write in this workbook

64. Reread your journal from your earliest entries. Write out your answers to the following questions about your patterns:

    1. What kinds of events are most likely to provoke negative feelings? Do these events happen most often when you are with other people or by yourself?

    2. What distorted thoughts show up repeatedly? Describe how your negative feelings build when you are thinking distortedly. What connection do you see between your most frequent feelings and your most frequent distortions?

    3. What are the negative payoffs you arrange to get? Which of your behaviors get you these payoffs? What distortions show up repeatedly in your journal to help you get the payoff feelings? What kinds of fantasies (for instance, sexually deviant, violent, or "getting back at") follow your payoff feelings?

    4. How often does your journal show you have carried out planning before an inappropriate behavior? How often do you interrupt your planning and choose a different behavior?

    5. As you read your journal entries from more recent days or weeks, do you begin to see a change in your pattern of reacting? If so, describe this change. If not, what distortions do you need to change to make new choices for your feelings and behaviors?

Continue to reread your journal every few weeks looking for patterns. Each time you will learn new things about yourself. Be especially conscientious in looking for change. Remember *improvement* is what treatment is about! ***Understanding is only useful if it helps you stop offending!***

Review your answers to this assignment with your therapist and your group. If you are working on your own, share your answers with a friend or person you trust.

18.

Journaling My Offense Cycle

THE DAY-TO-DAY AND WEEK-TO-WEEK PATTERNS you have recorded in your journal show how frequently you respond in the same ways to different events. This is your *style* of reacting. You use this same style of reacting in a more intense or exaggerated form when you are deep in your deviant cycle. Understanding the connection between your current patterns and your offense cycle is difficult, but it is necessary in order for you to break your cycle. You need to use all the ideas that were presented earlier in this volume and in SOS One and Two in making these connections.

It is a difficult task, but you are ready to work on a major assignment: journaling your offenses. This assignment helps you connect your behavior now and your behavior before and during your offenses. You need to share these journal entries with someone who understands your treatment. You should be able to talk with that person about the difficulties you encounter as you work on the task. You should work on the following assignments both now and long after you have completed reading this workbook.

Using your journaling techniques to look at your past offenses, you will break down the offenses into the same categories that make up your current daily journal entries: events and reactions. As you study the ways you reacted to the events leading to your offenses (your thoughts, body sensations, feelings, fantasies, and planning), you will learn how to identify and avoid the same patterns in the present.

Chapter 18 Assignment

 Do not write in this workbook

65. Using the list of your risk factors (Chapter Four, Assignment #23), search your journal to see when and how often they show up. Write in your notebook your answers to the following questions:
   1. How similar are the negative feelings you've recorded in your journal to the negative feelings you had when you were in your offense cycle?
   2. What thinking defects did you use to lead yourself deeper into your offense cycle?
   3. Which body sensations from your recent journal entries were also present when you were in your offense cycle?
   4. What thinking —> feeling —> behavior links appearing now in your journal are just like the ones right before or during your offenses?
   5. When you were in your deviant cycle, how did your planning lead you into acting on those fantasies? How is it the same now in your daily life?

6. In what ways are your daily behaviors still abusive (even if not sexual)? How are these similar to how you acted just before committing your offenses?

7. Record the events *leading up to* your most recent offense as if they had just happened. Begin at a time when you feel that you were not in your deviant cycle and work forward, including grooming (or stalking) your victim and your assault. For each event, record the feelings, body sensations, thoughts, fantasies, and planning you experienced then.

   If you *acted* on any deviant planning from one event, use that action as your next event. For example, suppose getting thrown out of a bar was an event leading up to your most recent offense. Enter that on the Event side of your journal as if it happened today. Record your thoughts, body sensations, thoughts, fantasies, and planning about having been thrown out of the bar. You may have *fantasized* about waiting for the guy you picked a fight with, beating him up, and taking his womanfriend away from him. You may have *planned* where you would wait and thought about getting something from the construction site across the street to use as a weapon.

   If you *acted* on these plans by going to the construction site to search for a two-by-four or a piece of pipe, record that as your next event, along with the thoughts, body sensations, feelings, fantasies, and planning that went with it. By entering the events in this way, you can recognize how your behavior moves in cycles.

8 What *risk situations* were you in during these events that you can now recognize and escape or avoid? Name the risk factors that have shown up in your journal entries of your most recent offense.

9. If you had more than one offense, repeat steps 7 and 8 for each offense, working backward in time from your most recent offense toward your first offense. What patterns or trends do you see developing in your offenses?

It will be helpful to your treatment if you share your answers to this assignment with your therapist and your group. If you are working on your own, share your answers with a friend or person you trust.

Endnote
You Can Stay Relapse Free!

YOU HAVE COVERED A LOT OF GROUND in this workbook. You have been introduced to the fundamentals of recognizing and changing your old patterns of behavior. You have learned how crucial it is for you to approach the work of self-change honestly and with determination. If treatment is available, you also have a therapist and/or a group to help you on the journey. At the very least, you should have close supportive friends with whom you can be completely honest.

This workbook has introduced you, as well, to a number of interventions—techniques you can use to change your thoughts, feelings, and fantasies. By now you should have a good sense of what your internal and external risk factors are and how to cope with them.

You also should be able to identify the Build-up, Acting-out, Pretend-normal, and Justification phases of your deviant cycle. The thinking and feeling links that make up these phases should be already show-ing up in your daily journal. Most important of all, you should now realize that *you must make the choice not to reoffend*. None of the intervention tools you have learned to prevent relapse will make a difference unless you use them.

You can succeed in moving from acting out deviant sexual behaviors to staying in control. You can build an offense-free life.

You may slip back into the old thoughts and feelings. Sometimes the old fantasies will find their way back into your mind. You will probably lapse and feel tempted to give in to the old patterns. *You always have a choice about whether to act out or not.* Remind yourself daily that you can make it.

The future can be better than the past when you work to make it happen. *Best wishes for courage, strength, honesty, determination, persistence, and confidence in building and maintaining your new, offense-free, victim-free life!*

Recommended Readings

Who Am I And Why Am I In Treatment? by Robert Freeman-Longo & Laren Bays (1988). The Safer Society Press, P.O. Box 340, Brandon, VT 05733. $10.95.

Why Did I Do It Again? by Laren Bays & Robert Freeman-Longo (1989). The Safer Society Press, P.O. Box 340, Brandon, VT 05733. $10.95.

Empathy & Compassionate Action by Robert Freeman-Longo, Laren Bays & Euan Bear (1996). The Safer Society Press, P.O. Box 340, Brandon, VT 05733. $12.00.

Men & Anger by Murray Cullen & Robert E. Freeman-Longo (1995). The Safer Society Press, P.O. Box 340, Brandon, VT 05733. $12.00.

Adults Molested As Children: A Survivor's Manual For Women & Men by Euan Bear with Peter T. Dimock (1988). The Safer Society Press, P.O. Box 340, Brandon, VT 05733. $12.95.

Macho: Is That What I Really Want? by Py Bateman & Bill Mahoney (1986). Youth Education Systems, Box 223, Scarborough, NY 10510. $4.75.

Out Of The Shadows by Patrick Carnes (1983). CompCare Publications, 2415 Annapolis Lane, Minneapolis, MN 55441. 1-800-328-3330. $8.95.

Victims No Longer: Men Recovering from Incest by Mike Lew (1988). Harper & Row, 10 East 53rd St., New York, NY 10022. $14.95 (paperback).

You Don't Have To Molest That Child by Timothy A. Smith (1987). National Committee for Prevention of Child Abuse (NCPCA), 332 S. Michigan Avenue, Suite 950, Chicago, IL 60604-4357. $2.00.

Men Surviving Incest by T. Thomas (1989). Launch Press, P.O. Box 5629, Rockville, MD 20855. $7.95.

Surviving With Serenity: Daily Meditations For Incest Survivors by T. Thomas (1990). Health Communications, Inc., 3201 S.W. 15th Street, Deerfield Beach, FL 33442. $6.95.

Secret Feelings And Thoughts by Rosemary Narimanian (1990). Philly Kids Play It Safe, 1600 Arch St., 8th Floor, Philadelphia, PA 19102-1582. $10.00.

Male Survivors: 12-Step Recovery Program For Survivors Of Childhood Sexual Abuse, by Timothy L. Sanders (1991). The Crossing Press, Freedom, CA 95019. (800) 777-1048.

For Guys My Age: A Book About Sexual Abuse For Young Men by Matthew Taylor (1990). Hawthorn Center, 1847 Haggerty Road, Northville, MI 48167. Free.

The Safer Society Program maintains nationwide information on agencies, institutions, and individuals identified as providing specialized assessment and treatment for youthful and adult sex offenders.

The Safer Society Program & Press
P.O. Box 340
Brandon, VT 05733
(802) 247-3132